Recollections of General Garibaldi I Rome to Lucerne • Elpis Melena

Publisher's Note

The book descriptions we ask booksellers to display prominently warn that this is an historic book with numerous typos, missing text or index and is not illustrated.

We scanned this book using character recognition software that includes an automated spell check. Our software is 99 percent accurate if the book is in good condition. However, we do understand that even one percent can be a very annoying number of typos! And sometimes all or part of a page is missing from our copy of a book. Or the paper may be so discolored from age that you can no longer read the type. Please accept our sincere apologies.

After we re-typeset and design a book, the page numbers change so the old index and table of contents no longer work. Therefore, we usually remove them.

Our books sell so few copies that you would have to pay hundreds of dollars to cover the cost of proof reading and fixing the typos, missing text and index. Therefore, whenever possible, we let our customers download a free copy of the original typo-free scanned book. Simply enter the barcode number from the back cover of the paperback in the Free Book form at www.general-books.net. You may also qualify for a free trial membership in our book club to download up to four books for free. Simply enter the barcode number from the back cover onto the membership form on the same page. The book club entitles you to select from more than a million books at no additional charge. Simply enter the title or subject onto the search form to find the books.

If you have any questions, could you please be so kind as to consult our Frequently Asked Questions page at www.general-books.net/faqs.cfm? You are also welcome to contact us there.

General Books LLC™, Memphis, USA, 2012. ISBN: 9781458965325.

PREFACE.

In these days of locomotive enterprise, a Lady's ride of some hundreds of miles does not excite much astonishment, and still less requires any apology.

Few, if any, will accuse her of unfeminine conduct in the desire to avail herself of a favourite exercise in combination with her wish to see the world; nor will many, it is hoped, be inclined to attribute to her any intention of making herself conspicuous by selecting a mode of satisfying her curiosity which; though not very common, is at least not without precedent, and such precedent as must prove it to be perfectly consistent with female modesty and ladylike manners.

Were it needful, I might instance the Author of " Letters from the South." Those who have read her work cannot but allow that it is quite a picture of amiable womanhood, and yet she stretched her equestrian wanderings as far as Asia Minor.

" A Ride through France and Italy " is not the work of a cavalry officer, but of a delicate, fair-haired daughter of England; and, look as closely as you may into its contents, you will not find a word or a thought inconsistent with her sex and station.

Have not Lady Sale, Lady Erroll, Mrs. Ford, and Mrs. Duberly made experience of equestrian, and even of warlike life, with honour, rather than stain, to their wife-like qualities?

I hope I may quote all these examples without meaning to compare my humble excursion to their more heroic deeds.

Whoever will venture to look into the stereoscope of these few leaves will, at most, find some Italian landscapes and a few character portraits, taken in the Romagna, the Marches of Ancona, and the beautiful valleys of Savoy; and I trust they will not be offended by some occasional notices of gratitude and affection to those two faithful four-footed servants to whom I owe much of the serene enjoyment of my journey.

DAYS ON HORSEBACK. CHAPTER I.
A RIDE FROM ROME TO LORETO.

" Der Fruiling ist die laute, die tonende, tauzendetimmige Naturperiode." rjIHE highest tree top on Monte Pincio had but just caught the first ray of the rising sun, when, on a bright May morning, I rode through the " Porta del Popolo," in company with some very dear friends.

Through the Via Flaminia, the little train made its way over the fragrant and still quiet Campagna. The splendid prospect, and the pleasant converse of friends, had made only *too* short the seven miles we had passed over, when we arrived at Prima Porta, the point at which those friends were to bid me farewell.

It was Ascension Day, a festival which made even this little collection of poor dwellings

B scarcely meriting the name of a town, look gay. Picturesque groups of peasants, who had come from far and near to celebrate the day, were kneeling at the open door of the small chapel, the narrow dimensions of which were quite insufficient for the concourse now assembled. Such a-devotional stillness reigned within the holidaydecorated walls, that the words of the officiating priest plainly reached our ears. The last " Ite missa est" was spoken; the dismissed congregation left the modest temple, the kneeling worshippers without arose, and not a few glances of curiosity and wonder were cast upon our little cavalcade.

On many a dull winter's day, on many a sunny spring evening, have I ridden through Prima Porta, little dreaming that this cold and lonely village, empty as it always appeared to me, could thus assume the pleasurable aspect which, under the influence of a brilliant morning and a few picturesque costumes and figures, it now wore.

The sudden sound of a bell close by me interrupted my reflections. My companions, notwithstanding the hour of the day, were determined to salute me with the discharge of a champagne cork! Each soon held in hand a glass of the sparkling beverage. Each drank heartily to my health and safe journey, and when their lips had drained the festive cup, the parting moment arrived.

A heartfelt " Lehewohl," and I rode on my way alone.

And now that my friends have left me, and that you, my dear reader, will henceforth be my sole companion, pardon me if I begin with a description of my escort! It is soon done, for it consists only of my Italian groom.

Giuseppe is not the man for a fine livery and white gloves, but a stout son of a rough peasant, born at Cori, and his career as a rider commenced in the ranks of the Papal dragoons. He will also do the duties of a house servant (for what will he not willingly do, except wear a livery?), but his present employment is more to his taste; and not only his blunt manner and soldier-like bearing, but also his proved probity, and his thorough knowledge of everything relating to horses, and above all, his excellent temper, make him invaluable to me, in such an expedition as the present.

The " Corese" is mounted on a stately roan, of the Pisan breed, whose courage and strength denote his fitness for a long march. As he brought his certificate of baptism with him into the world, in the shape of a large black mustache (an uncommon, but, it is said, indisputable mark of a good horse), it was impossible to name him otherwise than " Baffoni."

But my own beautiful sorrel, I must also introduce to you, who, not less fit for a journey than Baffoni, differs from him only in a finer form, and purer blood. His sire, a true Arabian, was said to be one of those which the Grand Seignor presented, some years ago, to the Holy Father. As soon as I became acquainted with the excellent qualities of this fine animal, I was inclined to call him " Tesoro;" but the firm and graceful manner in which he places his foot on the ground, and the elegance with which he holds his head and moves his body, insured him the less elegant, but more expressive, name of " Ballerino."

When I have told you of a graceful white Italian greyhound, which for beauty, fidelity, and understanding, is not to be matched, and her puppy of two months old, which I carry in a basket hanging from my saddle, I may close the catalogue of my four-footed companions.

An amplification of " Baffi "—mustache.

With this, my readers will be satisfied; but, to curious and suspicious police officers, who let nobody pass a gate without asking why, and whither, I must answer that I am going to Aix, in Savoy, for hygienic reasons. That I go by way of Loreto, may, perhaps, excite some surprise, but it will presently appear that I am not going there as a pilgrim. The riding habit is not quite an appropriate pilgrim's weeds, and my "Corese" does not look like a servant of the Church.

The visits of Pio Nono to the Marches of Ancona, and the Romagna, called universal attention to that fine but little known country, and also awoke in me the wish of seeing it. Only a few months before, I had witnessed the manner in which the Pope entered upon that journey, which led his unhappy subjects to combine with it such bright and bold hopes— for they thought he was going to open the prison doors, and to allow the poor " banished " to return home without fear. A terribly cold wind blew on that inclement morning, and not a single ray of the sun succeeded in piercing its way through the dark clouds. Under the escort of a host of cardinals and princes, marshals, noblemen, and full-dressed gendarmes, carriages with six horses, and fourgons with four, and almost over-ridden by his own "Guardia Nobile," the travelling equipage of Pio Nono rattled through the Porta Angelica. Far beyond the Ponte Molle, the people stood in double row, but not one " evviva " followed the departing monarch; the last spark of enthusiasm which he had raised ten years previously, having been long, long extinguished. Curiosity, and a sullen brooding over suppressed thoughts, spoke in every glance, as they gazed on a travelling cavalcade which looked more like a flight than a pilgrimage.

" Happy he," thought I at the sight, " who wears neither crown nor tiara, and who, unobserved and unconstrained, can sit on his horse and ride to a distant point; and still happier, if friendship have sped him on his way, and he have felt the parting pressure of the hand, and heard the hearty farewell." # # # #

I need not remind the reader that I started from Rome on the 21st of May for Loreto. I felt like one who has just received a long-wished for, but scarcely expected, book, and whose joy will not allow him to begin it methodically, although he anxiously glances through the leaves. The world seemed to lie open to me. That my horses should fall sick, or die—that the weather should prove adverse—that the rough mariners of my servant should get me into difficulties—that I might myself break down with the fatigue, all these appeared impossibilities. With the credulous confidence of La Fontaine's milkmaid as to the result of the sale of her commodity, I already wandered, in imagination, through all the most beautiful lands of Europe.—Switzerland, the Pyrenees, Spain and Portugal, were matters of certainty; and new pictures arose of distant zones, to which I was hastening with such celerity, that the milestones past which I rode were quite unheeded, until the sight of the obscure corner, called " Castel Nuovo di Porto " convinced me that I was still in Europe, even still in Italy, only eighteen miles from Rome, and that I must stop for breakfast.

The inn " Della Posta" is at the upper end of the winding main street. From this elevated site, the traveller's eye rests for the last time on the plains, and the classic ruins of the Campagna, Castel Nuovo lying on its most northern boundary: and here we must bid it farewell.

This clean and excellent hotel owes

its success chiefly to the circumstance of the town being the middle point between Rome and Civita Vecchia Castellana, and it is much frequented.

The road follows the direction of the Via Flaminia, and was, since Pius VI. formed a post road through Nepi, falling into entire neglect and disuse, and for its restoration the present Pope deserves our thanks. Finished but a few years ago, it is now used by all the vetturini going to Ancona, or to Florence by way of Perugia, as they gain by it the advantage of level ground and a diminution of distance.

As soon as the hot midday hours were past I again mounted, and proceeded onwards towards Civita Vecchia Castellana. The country now suddenly assumes an altered character. My eye sought in vain the prospects of the Roman Campagna, and must be contented with the narrow, fenced, cultivated landscape, over which spring was scattering the riches of her cornucopia. In the fragrant hedges appeared the blossoms of the wild rose, the honeysuckle, and the broom. In the shady clumps of southern trees, glistened the delicate green of the northern oak. The corn was already swelling into ear, and the scythe of the first mower was depriving the meadow of its luxuriant growth. An interesting animal world enlivened the picture: in lively gambols, untroubled by thoughts of the butcher's knife, the little lambs were bleating at their mothers' side; softly couched upon the turf, and little dreaming of the hardships that must follow this luxurious life, lay many a foal, under the watchful eye of its dam. From among the dark leaves, the earliest nightingales warbled forth their first serenade; and, browsing on the tender buds and young leaves, stood groups of goats, those classically renowned favourites of nature.

But it was not I alone who enjoyed this charming ride; my dog gave me notice of almost equal enjoyment, by coursing round me in wild ecstasy, now chasing a flight of young birds, now anxiously whimpering at the basket which contained her offspring, and then away she would run again.

Giuseppe seemed to be trying to overcome an unequivocal sensation of delight. The engrossing attention which preceded every, even an equestrian, journey, was over. In a comfortable state of carelessness, he held Baffoni back, in order that, at uninterrupted leisure, he might give his feelings full play. After we had ridden two miles at a fast pace, we passed the little town of Rignano, the birthplace of Cesare Borgia, which still at the present time gives a ducal title to one of the Roman princes. It lies seven miles from the mountain " San Martino," the site of the Etruscan city of Cagena.

The high road now winds along the foot of Soracte, or, as it is now called, "Monte Sant Oreste." The landscape becomes more interesting at every step, giving a foretaste of the splendid effects which attend a nearer approach to Civita Vecchia Castellana. The declining sun had not yet reached the horizon, and the purple gleams of his slanting rays lit up the mediaeval forms of the romantically situated city; approached by now broader and now narrower defiles, it rises upon a plateau of red volcanic tophus, having, phoenix-like, sprung from the ashes of the Etruscan city which is said to have been situated on the same spot, and which is at this time a welcome opportunity for disputation between the topographers and the archaeologists.

As I have no intention of adding to the number of superfluous " Handbooks for Travellers," or placing another " guide " in their already overloaded hands, I must be excused, if, while I wend my way down the serpentine road, I neither seek to explore the ruins of Etruscan walls, grave-like holes and hollows, nor the less massive constructions which lie among the rank thickets, but only try to give this general notion of the surrounding scene.

I dismounted at the Hotel della Posta, which is one of the best between Rome and Florence, and as soon as I had secured good quarters for my horses, I hurried towards the Citadel, in order to obtain a view of the fine prospect it affords, while yet under the effect of the setting sun.

The citadel is an octangular tower, surrounded by a triangular outwork, and stands upon an isthmus of land which joins the town with the higher ground; and besides the magnificent view which it commands, it offers, in the city prison, another object of curiosity to the stranger—Gasperone, the noted brigand, having been confined here for many years, and, as at his former prison in Civita Vecchia, the government allows him to receive the visits of strangers. The quickly approaching twilight had already done much to veil the view of the Tiber-washed Campagna, and the majestic Soracte, as I requested to be conducted to the cell of the grey-haired bandit chief.

A veteran Swiss who, like most of his class, had served under the great Napoleon, and told me many anecdotes of his eventful life, took me under his guidance, and after threading several empty corridors, we came to that wing of the building where Gasperone and his band were confined. The robber chief, surrounded by sixteen of his fellow convicts, who were whiling away the time in smoking and knitting, received me with visible self-conceit, which I scarcely expected from a man who had passed the first part of his life in reckless bloodshed, and the rest in disgraceful imprisonment; and as I contemplated his finely-formed head, his face, surrounded with silver hair, expressive and by no means vulgar; when I remembered that this man, after the death of his predecessor Cucumello, had been for six years the instigator, or executor, of every murder and robbery between Sant Agata and Fondi, (he himself boasting that he had slain " only " thirty of his fellow creatures with his own hand,) I felt that any faith I might have had in the philosophy of Lavater or Gall must be greatly shaken.

Gasperone told me that the Pope had offered him his freedom two years back, but that no mercy would be accepted by him, which was not extended to his companions. The whole establishment of this robber band did not give me at all an idea of a herd of malefactors deprived of their liberty, and might rather be Hkened to a company of travellers in quarantine. Of chains and gaolers I saw or heard nothing. The room was large, the beds good, and certainly in no German city society did the art of knitting ever flourish more successfully! The hands once used to the dagger and the pistol, now moved nothing but the innocent needle; one making a jacket, another a night-cap, and another a pair of pantaloons! Why, however, should not Gasperone enjoy all the advantages of his position? Are not, perhaps, the recollections and the exciting experiences of his first thirty years sufficient to make endurable a calm and undisturbed old age? The care of his Holiness for this hero of the Church States has gone so far as to allow him the use of tobacco and brandy, and bestowed on him a pension of two paoli a-day for pocket money! while a pious queen has added to the allowance, because the robber once commanded his band to rescue, in a night attack, the daughter of Maria Christina!

Oh! what an insight into world-governing charlatanism does not a visit to this hero of thirty murders give one! Here is this pensioned villain, sunning himself in comparative comfort, while untold numbers of guiltless victims of the cause of freedom pine in cruel dungeons, never to see the light of day, till that of their execution arrives! Does it not look as if a temporal judicature inquires not into the "quid," but only into the "quomodo" of all deeds?

The sun had risen but two hours when, the following morning, I pursued my wanderings, and the charms of the finely-cultivated country made me insensible to his glowing beams..

Borghetto, the first place I came to, is only a post station, with a few miserable houses around it, where the most easily satisfied of travellers could hardly take shelter for the night; but its picturesque situation and ruined castle (which stillin 1798,during the retreat of the French from Italy, was frequently garrisoned) must excite the admiration of all who see it. Close to Borghetto we find the "Ponte Felice," a beautiful bridge, built over the Tiber by Augustus Caesar, and restored by Sixtus V., joining Etruria and Umbria. A few miles onward we approach the village of Atricoli, occupying the site of the ancient "Ocriculum," the first place in Umbria which voluntarily submitted to the Roman yoke. In the year 1848, when a short-lived blaze of hope of freedom roused the Roman people into a sort of feverish energy and activity, they managed to make the Tiber navigable for small steamers as far as Ponte Felice; but the accommodation on board is so abominable, that it is only used by the common folk, and now and then some enthusiast artist—never by any more sensitive tourists.

After a hot ride of five hours I reached the old Umbrian town of Narni, which, placed on a hill, with its ancient tower and monastery, overlooks the valley of the Nera and its fruitful plain as far as the Apennines. The splendid bridge which Augustus Narni erected across the river has been celebrated by Martial in his epigram "ad Narniam."

" Sed jam parce niihi, nec abutere, Nanria, Quinto,
Perpetuo liceat sic tibi ponte frui."

Other authors have also spoken of its majestic arches, as being the most colossal of that time.

While the horses were enjoying their mid-day rest and refreshment, I followed the rugged road which lies between the town and the point where the Nera flows through the richly wooded valley till her wanderings join the Tiber. Here, where the imperial bridge once joined the two shores and carried the Via Flaminia over the river, the ruins of its massive arches span to this day a part of the stream. Only two arches on the right bank have succumbed to the effects of time. Surrounded by the beautiful scene, their ruins form an incomparable picture, while the fallen white marble blocks, unbesmeared with mortar, uninjured by iron cramps, lie at their foot in virgin purity.

Enraptured with the sight, and careless which way I went, I came unexpectedly upon the high road, where one of the triumphal arches lately raised in honour of the Pope's progress met my eyes, and brought me back from the past to the present. I will not trouble the reader with the bombastic Latin inscription which appeared on the face of this extemporaneous structure: I will only say that it was of classic style and unobjectionable proportions, and tastefully decorated. The only pity was that it was built of wood and canvas, and not of marble! One might have annihilated it with a blow!

Giuseppe met me, on my way to the inn, with the ill tidings that "Baffoni would not eat his provender!" I hastened to the stable, and found the poor beast with cold ears and staring eyes, and holding his head in a lifeless manner.

"Have you sent for a doctor?" said I.

"A doctor could do him no good, Signora. This illness, which probably will go off to-morrow, is but the consequence of to-day's long journey. My idea is to send the saddle-bags on by a vetturino to Terni, and that we should follow as soon as the horse is better; and there we shall find a better stable, and a doctor, if we want one."

This advice I took, and an improvement in the horse's condition soon enabled us to act upon it, though I could not shut my eyes to the fact that the sky was being overspread with clouds, and that a storm was far from unlikely.

We had proceeded only three miles from Narni, when the storm, coming from two opposite sides, met over our head. It hailed, it rained, it thundered, and it lightened, in so fearful a manner, that going onward was not to be thought of, and, indifferent whether it were hut or hovel, we sought the first building that was to be found. With that intelligence which all horses show in the time of danger, Ballerino and BafFoni hastened on, until we found ourselves in a walled building, where we could just hope to be kept from the hail and streaming rain.

In spite of the angry barking of dogs, and the screaming of disturbed fowls and their frightened progeny—in spite of the shrieks of flying children and their scolding mothers, we made good our entrance into the cottage, and found the needful shelter for ourselves and our horses. As the inhabitants soon discovered that we had none but peaceful intentions, they all came back together, and the universal uproar subsided into friendly t#lk, which (as never fails to be the case in Italy) ended in begging.

In about an hour the storm had spent its fury, but no friendly sunshine foretold a finer afternoon, and as, in my waterproof covering, I set forth again on my way to Terni, a more gentle, but continuous, rain fell, and the prospect of the beautiful valley through which I was riding was almost as effectually concealed from my eyes as a Turkish lady in a tashmac is from those of the public.

Night fell over us before we arrived at Terni, which, owing to its wool and silk fabriques, is a town of some magnitude. It is the successor of the ancient "Interamna," which gave the historian Tacitus to classical literature, and the rulers Tacitus and Florian to the Roman imperial dynasty.

At the Hotel della Posta I found a civil host and a good lodging; but it was not my object to remain there. The " Caduta delle Marmore " was known to me by a former visit, and it is not, I think, advisable to trouble my readers with another description of that often described wonder! Those who have read in the true spirit the glorious verses of Byron, in which he paints that " matchless and horribly beautiful cataract," may almost be said to have heard the hissing foam, and to have seen the tumult of the waters; to have wondered at the diamond world that sparkles beneath the Iris-bow which crosses the fall, and felt the cooling spray upon their cheeks.

The following morning relieved me much with respect to the horse's illness, for at five o'clock Giuseppe's rough knock at my door was followed by the pleasant news that " Baffoni was eating his food, and would soon be ready to travel." In less than an hour I was in my saddle; for though the breezy hills would leave little to fear from the heat, my day's work was likely to be a long one, and it was well to begin it early.

The first few miles carried me through the vale of Terni, with its luxuriant growth of vines, mulberry trees, and corn, as famous now as in the days of Pliny for its plentiful produce. But presently the country assumed a more alpine character. The road wound up picturesque hills, and the vegetation, constantly changing, presented an interesting variety to the eye. The swelling corn, the climbing vine, and the bushy mulberry, gave place to the sober olive, the dark mountain oak, and Erica bushes almost as large as trees, until at last only the strong oak and a few pines crowned the heights. As we approached nearer to Strettura, the singular form of " Monte Somma" came in sight. Strettura is a post station, near which is a large house, once the country residence of Leo XII. At the most elevated point of this pass, 3738 feet above the sea level, I enjoyed, through a clear atmosphere, an exceedingly fine view over the valley of Clitumnus, as far as Foligno and Spello, to which the rugged chain of the Apennines formed a worthy background.

None but the pedestrian or equestrian tourist can have the full benefit of so magnificent a scene as this. Every step he takes his attention is constantly occupied by undulations of ground, broken hills, winding roads, and changing vegetation; and during the long hours of his arduous walk he becomes intimately acquainted with the places he has struggled through, and arrives at last at the hard won height of the rough mountain top. It is then that he receives the reward of his toil, and feels his right to the enjoyment of the panorama beneath his feet. Then his breast may swell with pride, and

" Wo sein Auge schweift,
Wird ihm laut und schweigend kund
Das Leben der Natur.
Ihn ergreift
Unnennbar geistig wehen,
Als hört 'er den Gott durch die Schöpfung gehen,
Als sah er des Geistes verkörperte Spur."

The way down the Somma is very steep, but neither so long nor so wild as that to Terni; and at half-past ten I entered Spoleto, where we put up for our midday rest.

This is the "Spoletium" of the Romans, which, according to Livy, underwent an attack from Hannibal as he marched through Umbria, and which also suffered considerably during the civil war between Marius and Sulla. In the middle ages it rose to be a duchy, and annexed nearly the whole of Umbria to its territories; and even in the days of Hildebrand, in spite of the Countess Matilda of Tuscany having given it up to the Holy See, its municipal government was so well established, that the Pope was obliged to issue a special decree to deprive it of its privileges. In the year 1849 it served General Garibaldi as a bulwark to stop the progress of the Austrians.

The treasures of art contained in the church of Spoleto, the commanding site of its citadel, the ruins of a Roman theatre, and of the temples of Concord, Jupiter, and Mars, and the falling remains of a palace built by Theodosius; but, above all, the ancient aqueduct " Delia Torre," which serves also as a bridge—the rising ground on which the town stands, and the surrounding mountains—all these would require a much more elaborate notice than I can afford them here, but that most of my readers must be acquainted with them from other works.

A repetition of yesterday's storm rather damped my pleasure on my ride through the lovely vale of Clitumnus, the celebrity of which (as a talented English writer observes) has been immortalized by Virgil's verse and the Capitoline Triumphs—

" Hinc albi, Clitumne, greges et maxima taurus
Victima, saepe tuo prefusi fltunine sacro,
Eomanos ad templa Deum duxere triumphos."

Not far from the post station " Le vene," wells out of the Apennine chalk stone a fine stream of crystal clear water, and to the left a group of houses catches the eye; and here it is said the temple stood, dedicated to the river god Clitumnus, from whom both valley and river derive their name.

However fiercely the archaeologists and the scholars may argue the subject, the fancy of the traveller lingers fondly and believingly on a tradition which a Dryden, an Addison, and a Byron have adopted and celebrated.

Long did my eye rest on the ancient temple, now consecrated as the Church of San Salvadore, and on the classic stream which appears to be more interesting to the poet than the geographer. Byron could not refrain from singing its praise in his " Childe Harold," and the reader must excuse my refreshing his memory with the quotation—

" But thou, Clitumnus, in the sweetest wave
Of the most living crystal that was e'er
The haunt of river nymph, to gaze, and lave
Her limbs where nothing hid them; thou dost rear
Thy grassy banks, whereon the milk-white steer
Grazes; the purest gold of gentle waters, And most serene of aspect, and most clear;
Surely that stream was unprofaned of slaughters—
A mirror and a bath for Beauty's youngest daughters!
And on thy happy shore a temple still,
Of small and delicate proportions, keeps,
Upon a mild declivity of hill,
Its memory of thee: beneath it sweeps
Thy current's calmness; oft from out it leaps
The finny darter with the glittering scales,
Who dwells and revels in thy glassy deeps;
While chance some scattered waterlily sails
Down where the shallowor wave still tells its bubbling tales."

Those alone who know Italy well, can fully appreciate the life-like painting of the great poet. But who *does* know Italy well? Certainly not the travellers who, in closed caleche, with fleet post horses, gallop over its main roads, often passing the most beautiful parts in the darkness of night; and who, even in towns and cities, see nothing but what a tyrannic courier chooses them to see!

Oh! how delightful my independent mode, which allows me to linger over every beauty at my pleasure!

Time, and my wish not to overwork the horses, obliged me to abandon my idea of visiting the birthplace of Propertius; and it was quite evening before I reached Foligno, so repeatedly the scene of earthquake, and owing its reputation, as many Italian towns do, to a work of art — the " Madonna di Foligno," which was formerly in the Church " Delia Contessa," but is now in the Vatican.

The horse's illness still gave me much uneasiness, and the constant fear that I might be delayed, perhaps in some miserable little place among the Apennines, and indeed that my tour might be stopped altogether, had much shaken my intention of going across the Marches of Ancona and through the Ilomagna. Once or twice, indeed, I caught myself in the cowardly thought that it would be more advisable to go direct, by way of Perugia, to Florence! I was now, however, at a point where I must come to a decision. I dared no longer capitulate with myself; and as I mounted my horse next morning, it was determined. My love of enterprise did not desert me; and as soon as I saw the plains of Foligno behind me, and the new and interesting mountain passes which I was longing to explore before me—when I saw an Italian sky gleaming over a Swiss-like landscape, the last trace of fear left me, and the animated pace of my horses banished every thought of hesitation from my mind. The Pass of Colfiorito exceeded in grandeur and wildness many a more celebrated one, and had deeper clefts, narrower valleys, and finer prospects than could be expected from its moderate height. In winter, its roads c must be dangerous, if not impassable, from snowdrifts. A small lake which we found nearly at its summit, and not far from Colfiorito, instead of producing trout, is famous for leeches, which, though probably a more advantageous property for the dwellers in that town, are not so grateful to the visitor who arrives there with the famishing effects of the mountain breezes apon him.

Our road now wound along the rapid " Chienti," the source of which is not far from Serravalle, and which then pursues its course of fifty-eight miles to Civita Nuova, in the Adriatic Sea. The valley soon increases in breadth, and the hills recede, and several romantically placed villages adorn their last slopes. A sabbath-like rest reigned over nature and man. Holiday-clad peasants animated the winding paths of this smiling neighbourhood. From the open village church issued the sounds of a fine organ. Its lengthened tones harmonized sweetly with the nightingale's song and the joyful laugh of children. The pleasure I felt was increased by the fact that the journey had done the horses no harm, and I greeted with much satisfaction the village host, as he came forward with an offer of good quarters for the night.

I soon discovered, however, that I was not in the land of Canaan. Hardly a crust of bread was to be had, and in vain did Giuseppe run about in search of oats. All that remained for us was to make our stay as short as possible. At four o'clock, therefore, next morning—unrefreshed by much beyond sleep and rest—we again started, and a bitter cold wind was no very agreeable accompaniment to our ride to Tolentino, a small town, interesting to Catholics as the scene of the life, death, and miracles of St. Nicolas, and to the historian as the place where the treaty between Pius VI. and Buonaparte was concluded in 1797.

The Gothic gateway of Tolentino is much admired as a well-preserved specimen of mediaeval architecture. The landscape also improved with every step after passing the town; and as the deserted fortress of " La Rancia" met my eye, the historical recollections attaching to it soon dissipated all thoughts of fatigue and selfdenial. It was here, on the banks of the Chienti, that the bloody but decisive encounter between Murat and the Austrians took place, on the 2nd May, 1815. When the King of Naples heard of Buonaparte's return from Elba, he advanced with 40,000 men, by way of Rome, Florence, and Modena, and, without plan or means, he began hostilities against the Austrians. He reckoned on the help of the French, but it never came! Beaten by the Austrians on the 12th April, near Ferrara, he pursued the road that led him to La Rancia, where his already depressed army was again beaten and dispersed. Murat himself was very nearly taken prisoner. By a very ill-considered manoeuvre of one of his generals, his best position had fallen into the possession of the enemy, and his whole army had been thrown into confusion. To use the words of Colletta, insubordination had long had the upper hand. Against the misfortunes of that day, Murat's own personal courage was of no avail. Disobedience frustrated all his plans, and corruption had extended through all his ranks. With enormous loss he had to retreat to Macerata, whence he saw himself obliged to retrace his way to Naples with the remnant of an army which never was worthy of his military genius. Fate still followed the unfortunate King, who fled from Naples a few weeks afterwards, and a few months later his honourable career was closed in the most tragical, if also heroic, manner, in the prison of Pizzo!

Long before you reach Macerata you obtain a view of it, proudly placed as it is on an insu« lated hill, between the Apennines and the Adriatic. The increasing interest of the scenery shortened the last part of our long ride, for it was nine o'clock, and consequently five hours, before I dismounted at the Hotel della Pace. With much satisfaction I established my horses in a capital stable, and after seeing them (as I always do) plentifully fed, I hastened into the hotel to enjoy, myself, all the refreshments of civilization and comfort. It was my intention to remain here but a few hours, and to get through the remaining eighteen miles to Loreto the same afternoon; but, after taking a good breakfast and a short siesta, and then a stroll through the town, on looking into the stable I saw that the horses would be so much better for a longer rest, that I postponed my departure till the following morning.

I had no cause to repent this resolution, for the charming position of this pleasant town really deserves the travellers notice. I think I could even recommend it to the blaze tourist, as a place for a summer's residence. Its fine palaces and churches—the architecture, particularly of that of the Madonna—the carved woodwork in the cathedral, and a painting ascribed to Perugino,—all had a share of my admiration; but what delighted me as much as anything was an undulating path which afforded a promenade round the town, and an incomparable panorama. From this path the eye wanders from the snow-capped Apennines to the shore of the Adrian Sea, over a lengthened landscape, which appears to contain everything that belongs to European scenery—numberless heights crowned with villages and monasteries and towns, river-watered meadows and fruitful vales, wooded hills and cultivated plains. I tortured my memory a long time to see if I could call to mind any prospect I could compare to this; and, though Switzerland wants the beautiful adjunct of the sea, I think the French Cantons the only part of Europe which can be thought to approach it in loveliness and variety.

This rare view is especially fine towards the north-east. Not far from the sea a glimpse may be caught of a part of Loreto, with the dome of its church of " Santa Casa." A number of towns, amongst which Recanati, Osimo, and Fano are the most important, are so plainly visible, that I seemed to have a stereographic map stretched out before me. I found it difficult to tear myself from it; and the sun had set for some time, and twilight had a little confused the fair picture (which to my fancy made it all the more enchanting), before I left it to return to my inn.

Neither the hammer of the early smith, nor the first cry of the "Acquavitaro," broke the silence of the morning, as, a short while before daybreak, I left Macerata, and softly fell, the steps of the horses on the pavement of the death-like streets. But soon the first streaks of dawn appeared to light our winding way; and as we reached the foot of the hill, both the nightingale and the lark saluted us with their melodious tones.

Recanati, which, according to the result of research, occupies the place of " Helvia Ricina," founded by Septimius Severus, stands, like Macerata, on an insulated hill, and presides over a prospect which some have thought to surpass that of the sister town. This town, however, possesses a greater interest for me on other grounds. It was the birthplace of Leopardi. Few, I fear, of my readers may know this name, but Italy pronounces it with pride. Alike eminent as poet, linguist, and philosopher—great through the admirable gifts of nature, great through intense study, great through the modesty and purity of his life— Leopardi would have ranked among the first, not only of Italy's, but of Europe's, celebrities, had he not been snatched away by a premature death. Neither the love and care of the most devoted friends—not the soft air of Tuscany or the enchanting neighbourhood of the Neapolitan Gulf—could stay the inexorable hand of Death. He was delicately formed, and had been sickly from his youth, and he became the victim of consumption before he had completed his fortieth year. At Capo di Monte his dear friend Antonio Ranieri received the last sigh of this accomplished man, of whom a German poet has said, "Jene grosse Italienische Poesie, die auf Dante's Lippen geboren wurde, auf den seinigen gestorben sei!"

Whoever is familiar with the works of a poet or a thinker, must feel interest in the place (even if entirely void of beauty) of his birth or his childhood, and even of his after years, as these places must have contained the materials for those impressions on his mind which produced his works. The sight of the objects which animated Leopardi to the composition of his " Canti," and called forth his earnest " Pensieri Morali," could not be indifferent to me; for in the unbounded sea, from whose waves he had so often watched the rising of the moon—a favourite subject of his Muse—in the distant points of the

Apennine mountains, and in the smiling landscape between, I recognized the scene of his labours and the subjects of many of his sketches. Leopardi had prepared himself for life as for a festive day. Upright, humane, liberal, and high-minded himself, he expected to see in others the reflection of his own virtues, until, betrayed and deceived by those in whom he placed most faith, he fell into the opposite extreme, and entertained the sad creed that mankind were all bad alike! A noble spirit like his could never have been long so impressed, and it cannot but be supposed that a few more years of life would have led him to a better and sounder philosophy.

A few miles only divide Recanati from Loreto. A fine aqueduct, erected by Paul V., stretches its length from hill to hill, over the intermediate valley. A heavy rain as I entered the city determined me to devote the day to this far-famed resort of pilgrims, and, entering the narrow main street, I dismounted at the Hotel " La Campana." CHAPTER IL LA SANTA CASA DI LORETO.

" Ecco fra le tempeste e i fieri venti
Di questo grande e spazioso mare,
0 Santa Stella, il tuo splendor m'ha scorto;
Che illustra e scalda pur l'umane menti;
Ove il tuo lume scintillando appare,
  E forge al dubbio cor dolce conforto
In terribil procella, ov'altri e morto:
E dimostra co'raggi
1 sicuri viaggi,
  E questo lido e quello, e'l polo, e'l porto
Della vita mortai ch'appena varca,
Anzi sovente affonda,
In mezzo l'onda,
Alma gravosa e carca."

As soon as I had chosen my rooms in the Hotel Campana (not a very firstrate one), I set off to visit the Cathedral, in order to see the " Santa Casa," or " Holy House," of which it has been the blessed possessor for upwards of 500 years, and which is by far the most famous sanctuary and resort of pilgrims in all Catholic Christendom.

Devout popes and ambitious kings have helped to increase the store of "ex votos" which its renown has collected upon its altar, from the extremest confines of the Christian world.

The little town of Loreto was originally called " Villa di Santa Maria;" afterwards, " Castilla di Santa Maria;" and its present appellation is derived either from the Grove of Laurels near the place where the " Holy House " first rested in Dalmatia, during its transportation from the East, or else from a rich and noble lady, by name Laureta, to whom that laurel grove belonged.

That this holy building was bodily lifted up and borne by angels from Galilee to Tersati in Dalmatia, in the year 1291, and three years later safely carried to Italy is a well-known legend! But as with many travellers it has happened, so did it with this aeronautic house, that the journey itself went smoothly enough, but its arrival was not without difficulties and dangers. Perhaps it will not be unwelcome to the reader if I give a literal extract from an account written by a " faithful" narrator! " Like as it was first permitted to shepherds to behold the glory of the manger in Bethlehem, so also was it reserved for other simple shepherds, as they ' watched their flocks by night,' on the shores of the Adriatic, to have the first glimpse of the 'Santa Casa.' Dazzled by an unusual light which shone over the sea upon the Laurel Grove of Recanati, they went to look what it could be. What was their surprise, when on a spot where never trace of building was seen before, they found the object on which the luminous rays converged, to be a small dwelling! The poor men were lost in wonderment and conjecture, until one of them declared that he ' had seen it borne along by angel hands from far beyond the sea;' and then, persuaded that it must be the work of God, they passed the rest of the night in contemplation and in prayer. At the first appearance of dawn, the shepherds hastened to the town to relate to their several masters what they had beheld. The undissembled joy which beamed on the countenances of these simple folk, the plainness of their narrative,, and the exact accordance of the story of each with the others, seemed to banish all thought of deception, and the citizens followed them in troops to the Grove, to obtain ocular conviction of a fact so apparently incredible. The ancient style of the building, the unusual decorations, the firmness with which, without any foundation, it rested on the ground; its little altar surmounted by a cross, and the graceful but majestic figure of the Madonna, filled the beholders with such reverence that the tears fell from their eyes, and between fear and joy they cried out that the hand of God was in it, and that the building could be nothing short of heavenly and holy!

" The Madonna was not slow to fix the faith of her children. That same night she appeared to all the friars of the Augustine order of St. Nicholas of Tolentino, and others then established at Recanati, and assured these faithful servants that the house was actually the dwelling she had occupied in Nazareth, and that it had been transported hither to do honour to the town of Loreto.

"The news of this wonder spread over the land with the celerity of lightning, and all places around rang with the fame of the ' Selva de Laureta,' and the Santa Casa di Nazaretta. Pilgrims of all ages, of every race and every class, flocked to the Grove by day and by night, eager to see the miracle with their own eyes. The richest and most delicate hesitated not to exchange the luxuries of home for the rough ground of the Wood, whence now issued a perpetual chorus of mingled prayers and praises and thanksgiving!

" Some foolish men, however, actuated more by devilish instigation than rapacious desires, dividing themselves into different bands, attacked the pilgrims with violence, and put them in such alarm, that the concourse decreased by degrees, and soon afterwards entirely dispersed.

"This, however, occurred only with the permission of Heaven, and in order to strengthen the faith of the devout by a fresh miracle. For eight months after its first arrival, the ' Santa Casa' raised itself again, and settled down on a pleasant hill about a mile from the Laurel Grove. This spot was the property of two peaceable brothers, who, rejoiced at the gift thus bestowed on them, set themselves earnestly to pay it every possible honour; but in a few days the altar and the walls were so covered with costly gifts and countless offerings, that envy and avarice filled their hearts, and they were not far from staining the sanctified floor with brotherly blood. To prevent such a catastrophe, the holy house again removed about a gunshot farther, to the place where it has now stood since 1295!

" When the inhabitants of Recana.ti saw the

Heaven-brought building rest on their ground, they determined to surround it with outer walls, which might protect it from the weather and all other dangers. Covered ways also for the pilgrims, and houses for officiating priests, formed a part of the design; and before long the plan was extended to the erection of a splendid church over the Santa Casa! With this fabric the concourse of visitors, and the houses required for their use, increased so greatly, that Sixtus V., in 1586, raised Loreto to the dignity of a city, and fortified it with walls to protect it from the Turkish pirates, who, allured by the treasures it contained, often made incursions on the coast. Under the same pope, and, indeed, but a few years after this, the cathedral was completed, and on its facade is a black marble tablet, on which is written in golden characters:—

" Deiparse Domus in qu& Verbum Caro factum est." »#

So far the old chronicler! The square in which I now found myself was enclosed on one side by the monastery of the Jesuits, and on the opposite side by the palazzo of the governor, a fine building from the design of Bramante. In the centre stands a bronze statue of Sixtus V., and a third side is occupied by the cathedral. One willingly overlooks its tasteless front in order to gaze with admiration upon its three bronze doors, which surpass in beauty those of Pisa. They are of the sixteenth century, and the work of the best masters. The bas-reliefs on them contain subjects from the New Testament and from the Old, surrounded by arabesque borders, &c.

But it would be a departure from my plan, were I to enlarge on the mass of treasures— in silvam ne ligne feras. The masterpieces of a Guido, a Domenichino, a Baroccio, a Carracci, which are here repeated in mosaic; the frescos of Zuccari, or a Luca Signorelli, and a Pietro da Cortona; the sculptures of a Calsagni and a Benedetto de Majano: all these offer a rich repast to the beholder, but scarcely to the distant reader.

But of the " Santa Casa " itself, which, after all, is the most interesting object of the church, I cannot refrain from indulging in a few words more.

It is a small house, built of common brick, and with very moderate art. Its height is about 15 feet, its length about 32 feet, and its breadth 13£ feet. On the north side there is a door, and on the west a window, over which is an antique cross. The original floor is wanting. It was lost, they tell you, in its wonderful passage from Nazareth. It is now paved with quarries of red and white marble. The entire structure is enclosed in a kind of case of beautifully wrought marble, the walls being covered with superb bas-reliefs by Bramante. It is a complete museum of art treasure, and of rich detail, for the mere inspection of which hours, and for the full examination of which days, would be necessary. It is, as an enthusiastic writer has called it, an " Opera Divina," to the finishing of which 60,000 scudi would have been inadequate, but that many of the artists and artisans gave their assistance without pay or reward.

In a niche over the fireplace stands the celebrated statue of the Virgin. It is said to have been carved out of cedar of Lebanon, by St. Luke. Through age, it is now nearly black. The figure of the Virgin, as well as that of the infant Saviour, is brilliant with precious stones, glittering in the light of a silver lamp kept perpetually burning upon the altar. Two earthen jars, said to have been used by the holy family; a stone, which the bishop of Coimbra took away in the time of Paul III., but afterwards restored, because while it was in his possession his health failed him! a cannon ball, which the warlike Julius II., remembering his preservation from the attack of Mirandola, vowed to the Virgin; costly presents from Prince Hompesch, the Grand Master of the Knights of Malta—and from the Polish family of Plata von Wilna—these are but a few of the treasures and relics, though perhaps the most notable, and worthy of recording.

Scarcely a year had elapsed after the Tolentine treaty of peace when the French took possession of Loreto, and carried the statue over to Paris. It is well known that they deposited it in the coin room of the great library, where, placed immediately over a mummy, it was exhibited to the public as one of the curiosities of that learned collection. In 1801 it was restored to Loreto, though some doubts have been raised as to its authenticity.

In the great chapel where the church treasure is deposited, there was the richest assemblage of costly offerings which the devotion, or the policy or pride, of the world ever brought together. Popes and prelates, monarchy and princes, joined in adding to the store; but the misfortunes of the unequal war between the Papal States and the French obliged Pius VI. to make use of this wealth in order to satisfy the exactions made at the peace. But there is one offering, of which neither robbery nor war can deprive the Madonna di Loreto, and which possesses a more unfading brilliancy than all her jewels—the magnificent canzone which the great singer of the " Jerusalem Delivered" composed to her honour, when, in the year 1587, he passed through the city on his way from Bologna to Rome. Let those who are skilled in Italian not content themselves with the few lines which head this chapter, but study the whole poem, from which breathes that elevated devotion which religion only could inspire.

After the re-establishment of peace, immense effort was made to replace these losses, and contributions from all nations again embellish the walls and fill the cabinets.

The eyes of the sober-minded Protestant wander in mute bewilderment over these valuable gifts, which originate not in heathenish times, or in the superstitious middle ages, but in the first half of the enlightened century in which we now live, and are still, from day to day, receiving the additions which pious pilgrims make to them.

The sacristan who conducted me round the church, mentioned the circumstance of a daring robbery which had been committed in it some years back, and laid much stress on the great cunning and courage evinced by the perpetrator of it, seeming to think more of his cleverness than of the sacrilegious nature of the act. "Ungran fatto davvero!" he exclaimed more than once, and he called the thief "un gran Filosofo," telling me that he now lives at liberty in Loreto, and is named by the people " II Dottore," and enjoys general respect.

On my way home to my hotel, I saw the figure of a grey-headed old man, who, in spite of the poverty of his appearance, did not ask alms of any one. A poor man who does not beg is a thing so rare in this country, that the one before me was doubly an object of curiosity, and I could not help inquiring who he was. " That is ' II Dottore,'" said mine host, with a look full of meaning.

This repetition of the name made me think to myself " Why should not I shorten a dull evening by making acquaintance with this celebrity? " of whom indeed I had already heard in Rome, and who was spoken of as a kind of juridical curiosity, who, in spite of a conviction for sacrilege, enjoyed his freedom and universal respect!

After entering my room I sent for the landlord, and asked if he thought the Doctor would have any objection to relate to me his history.

" None in the world," he replied, " particularly if you place before him a bottle of good wine—and a more interesting story the Signora is never likely to hear."

" Well then," said I, " let him be sent for, and let it be your care that neither good wine nor a good supper be wanting."

In less than an hour the robber of the church entered my apartment. What a phrenologist would make of his head I know not, but upon me the Doctor made no unfavourable impression. He was of the middle height, bent more by suffering than the weight of years. The regular form of his features, the fire of his eyes, the full growth of hair, which hung from his lofty forehead, showed me what he must have been in his youth. His manners were good, and he greeted me without any constraint.

When he had refreshed himself with the. collation set before him, he took up the half emptied " Fiasco," filled his glass, and began what he called the story " delle mie disgrazie.

As a typical picture of Italian character, it seemed to me so peculiar and so interesting, that I venture to lay it before my readers, just as I heard it from the mouth of my visitor.

CHAPTER III. IL DOTTORE.
A TEUE NARRATIVE.

"notwithstanding the poverty-stricken and neglected condition in which you now see me, Signora," began the Doctor, in a lamentable tone, " I am of a wealthy and much respected family: my parents were landholders, who cultivated their own estate, and at the time of my birth my father filled the honourable post of a ' Perito della comune e della Santa Casa.'

" Nevertheless, I cannot deny that, from what I have discovered of my forefathers, I must come to the conclusion that they were always distinguished by a great love for their neighbours' property. There are families in

Perito signifies a sort of councillor. whose blood this peculiarity seems to be inherent. The Secretary of State, His Eminence the Cardinal Antonelli, occurs to my mind as a case in point. The same propensity which has elevated him to so high an office, has kept his near relative Gasperone in contumelious captivity. The cleverer of the two selected the Church— studied hard, and devoted all his energies to the attainment of a prelacy, and, favoured as much by circumstances as inclination, he reached every point he proposed to himself ' dove si ruba al tavolina' cioe ' a coperto e con onore;'f while his cousin, less endowed with ambition, industry, and luck, took to the highway, where robbery and murder are not so prolific of honour and reward, To what end was the poisoning of a whole band of brigands at Urbino? To See "lie Gouvernement Pontifical, ou la Question Italienne," par Edmond About, chap. 11. f Where a man may sit at his writing-desk, and rob with security and honour. A band of thirty robbers had ensconced themselves upon a hill near Urbino. The Duke caused some mules laden with provisions to be driven that way, which, of course, the robbers seized upon. The provisions were poisoned, and the wretched plunderers died on the spot. '' When the news reached Sixtus V.," says a writer, " the Pope experienced much satisfaction." what end the cruel severity of Sixtus V.? the subsequent hunting of the rest of the band, the high price put on the heads of their leaders, the disgraceful execution of Giovanni de Pepoli?

" It is true that Marco Sciarra, and many other robber chiefs, evacuated the Papal States for a time, and that Prete Guercino, Fara, and others perished; but in a country where neither an openly political life, nor any participation in the government—where neither army nor navy offer to strong and energetic youth a legitimate field for the employment of their talents— where the management, or rather the mismanagement, of the education of the rising nobility is entrusted to an enervated and demoralized priesthood, whose sole object is to keep them in ignorance and superstition, in order that they themselves may the more luxuriously recline upon the down of slothful ease, at the physical and moral expense of the people—in such a land, brigandism must, and will, be the favourite field of action for young and restless bravery.

" But let me return to the period of my birth, which, if I do not mistake, was the 7th January, 1794.

" Of my early youth I have nothing of import

D ance to relate. As soon as I could escape from maternal care and supervision, I accompanied my father upon his tours of inspection over our estate, and while he superintended the work of the labourers.

" Later on, with my parents' permission, I devoted a portion of my time to the care of the altar in the church of ' Santa Casa.' This occurred partly in consequence of the office which my father held as ' Perito' often taking him to the cathedral, and partly because my parents had the intention of dedicating me to the Church, a project the non-fulfilment of which I have often lamented, because, as I have said before, a priestly life is the only one, in my unhappy country, where talent and acuteness can hope for a brilliant career.

" I grew up, like the majority of my equals, in unmanly, inactive neglect. My "indolence and my love of pleasure, qualities which so strongly characterise our southern organisation, were great; but if they had been restrained at this time, it is not improbable that the high capacities with which nature had endowed me might have been developed. It scarcely beseems the old man bent down with the weakness of age, heavy trials, want, and distresses of every kind, to boast of the graces of his youth, but nevertheless, Signora, if you could ask one of my former companions what Dr. Vincenzo was fifty years ago, you would be told of his handsome countenance, and his statue-like figure, and that the elegance of his movements and his noble bearing, his ever ready wit, and his bold extravagance, made him the favourite of every feast, and the chosen model of all the fair youth of Loreto and its neighbourhood! It was not long that the power of love lay dormant in my breast, but it was not any of Loreto's daughters, but Vittoria of Recanati, whose beauty pierced my heart. Accompanied by her parents, she came every festival day to our church to attend mass. It was there I first saw her, there that I watched her in silent homage. Oh! Signora! how vividly lives the memory of those happy moments in my soul!— until, beneath the snow-white cloth, which according to the country fashion covered the small head of the lovely girl, her eyes half closed with maiden modesty, devotion, and the first gleams of love, gave me an encouraging sign of mutual intelligence.

" From that day forward my constant steps were turned towards Recanati. Vittoria's parents, flattered at the idea of having me for their son-in-law, soon gave their consent; and as my own were also anxious that their wild Vincenzo should, by an early and happy union, be "Yeaned from his military inclinations, and preserved from further irregularities, every impediment was smoothed down, and before I had completed my nineteenth, and Vittoria her seventeenth year, we offered our marriage vows before God's altar.

" Quiet domestic happiness could not satisfy my wild desires. Scarcely was the first intoxication of love and the novelty of married life over, than I commenced a career of excess and intrigue, to which my youth and personal charms, my easy position, and my happy assurance, all combined but too strongly to tempt me.

" With a hearty embrace, I tried to propitiate my pouting bride; with a boyishly lavish caress, I lit up the darkened countenance of my offended mother, in order that I might plunder her storecloset with less compunction; with a timely jest, I turned aside my father's wrath, with a view to a larger participation in his wealth: in short I was one of those favoured few, to whom everything is forgiven, and from whom everything is borne. It was not long, however, before my inordinate desire of gain, my measureless pride, and my wish to appear richer than I was, induced me to have recourse to play. My nights were, for the most part, spent with young men with the same propensities, and I seldom reached home before daybreak. Neither the righteous reproofs of my father, nor the ardent entreaties of my mother, nor the tears of my suspicious wife, could bring back my heart to better thoughts, or myself to a more honourable course of life.

" Notwithstanding my heartlessness and frivolity, I could not be blind to the sorrow which was blenching the still beautiful countenance of my poor mother. For some time I had remarked how diligently she had been seeking for some opportunity to speak with me alone, and knowing well that such an interview could bring me nothing but well-deserved reproaches, I succeeded, for some time, in preventing it; but one morning, as I returned, at my now usual hour of day-break, from a gambling and drinking party, I found the house-door open, and my pale mother, looking like a ghost, in wait for my arrival.

"In the most affectionate manner she began by representing to me into what an abyss of misery my known course of life would plunge me and my whole family. In the most affectionate manner she then entreated me to retrace my steps, and to become again a blessing to my parents, the happiness of my wife, and an example to my children. At no time, however, could her well meant homily have come so *mat apropos,* for, annoyed and irritated by a heavy loss at play, I met it with scorn, and the consequence was, that my mother's loving entreaties were turned into wrathful indignation. She seemed changed into an enraged tigress, her anger knew no bounds, a stream of the heaviest curses flowed from her lips, and according to our land-custom, stretching her arm over the blazing fire of the hearth, she invoked the holy St. Antonio to send down the just vengeance of heaven upon the head of her son!

"From that very moment,"continued the Doctor, after a short pause, and with a tone of earnestness that showed he had closed the happy part of his life, " began my heavy fate! The curse of a mother was upon me! What then could save me? My drinking companions insulted me; my luck at the gaming table deserted me; even the female sharers of my sins were faithless.

" An occurrence of little importance in itself raised me from this miserable condition, and awoke in my unsatisfied breast emotions which incited me to the undertaking of great deeds.

" Among our people there was a young man whose name was Anto, and who had served many years on our farm. It was not unknown to me that small thefts had taken place on our estate, and that the same thing had occurred on neighbouring properties—fowls, pigeons, fruit, in short, almost everything that is usually met with on a farm, and is easily carried away. I fixed my attention on this same Anto, and as I observed that, during the hot weather, he took rather too long a repose, it struck me that perhaps his nights were more wakeful, and probably devoted to his depredations.

" My watchful and continued strictness did not at all please him. ' Sir,' said he, one day, ' what is the cause of your altered behaviour towards me? Why do you look on me with less good-will than heretofore?' ' Because you are ungrateful and foolish,' I replied. ' Ungrateful, because you are robbing your employer; and foolish, because you are running the risk of the galleys for a few trumpery birds and such like. The whole world is open to you; cannot you exercise your talents, which are so remarkable, somewhere else, and steal in a manner that will make you rich, powerful, and famous?'

"' Ah! believe me, Sir,' said Anto, ' that if I were in your case, and had admittance everywhere, I would do many cunning tricks. How often, when I have seen you go up the steps of the counting-house, have I not said to myself that one good opportunity should make me rich and powerful!'

"Anto's words fell on my soul as a ray of light, and suddenly awoke my slumbering impulses. I felt the existence of those qualities which, as I have said already, existed in the character of my forefathers, and these qualities were soon to bear dreadful fruits.

" My relation towards Anto was henceforward changed. He saw in me no longer the suspicious, stringent master, but a mighty leader, through whom he was to become the possessor of enormous wealth; and he was no longer in my eyes the cowardly thieving servant, but one of my most devoted comrades!

" My life began to be distinguished now by activity and enterprise. In concert with Anto, I turned my attention first to the money chest of Santa Casa.

" While my accomplice remained at the foot of the staircase to warn me of any approaching danger, I hastened up, forced open the first door, and entered the strong room. So far, all went well. But, unfortunately, the high expectations we had entertained of the amount of the booty were deceived, for, instead of the considerable sum which we hoped to find, and which probably had only been lately removed, we discovered but a few thalers—a miserable reward for our daring undertaking!

"Far, however, from being discouraged by this failure, we only thought of greater enterprises, and heated our imagination with the invention of hazardous plans, until at last we came to the heroic thought of despoiling the Madonna of the money which had been offered at her shrine. Does the image eat or drink, that it requires all this money?' asked I of Anto, as he seemed rather to tremble at this contemplated sacrilege. ' Did not Napoleon commit many scandalous robberies without consideration or remorse? Did he not deprive emperors and kings of their thrones, wives of their husbands, mothers of their sons, and children of their fathers? The blood of all Europe was hardly enough to satisfy this vampire, and yet he is the idol of men! Whose rights are we invading? Whom are we condemning to poverty? Whose tears are we drawing forth, if we put this money, which never can do any good to an image, to useful purposes V

"These fine arguments so enlightened my comrade, that I completely won him over to my way of thinking, and he promised to stand by me truly in this great enterprise. The money which we contemplated appropriating was kept in a chamber in the inmost part of the church, and it required no little exercise of ingenuity and forethought to execute our design.

" Accompanied by my wife, who was properly tutored, I sat me down, one bright afternoon, on the steps of the hospital, which was situated behind the back part of the cathedral, and exactly over against that part which I had selected as being the most suited to my purpose. Apparently with no other intention than to enjoy the sunshine, I began to count the courses of stone in the high wall before me, from the bottom to the top; and when this was done, I measured with my outstretched thumb and fingers the exact height of each course.

" Armed with these two data, I easily calculated the height of the entire wall, and now all depended on my being able to procure a ladder of sufficient length to reach the cornice with which the wall was surmounted. Certain repairs which happened at that time to be going forward favoured my plans, and I had only to find where the masons placed their ladders when they left off work for the day. The breaking open of the shed where they lay was the first step in my great work, and it was accomplished in one dark December night in 1826.

" The ladder we thus secured was not quite long enough, but with the addition of a long and strong pole, it enabled us to mount the wall.

" Everything went prosperously forward. Having reached the highest point of the wall, with one or two blows of the hand we broke the glass of a window, and let ourselves down into the church by means of a knotted rope. A few minutes more placed the money in our grasp, and this time the booty even exceeded our hopes. The gold and silver coins were carefully tied up in two sealed bags, which made it very easy to carry them off. However, the incense-charged atmosphere of the place, the holy stillness which reigned amongst the timehonoured arches, even the look of the revered Santa Casa itself, had such an effect on Anto's courage, that at the very moment when he was about to ascend the rope with a part of our prize, his strength utterly forsook him. In vain were all my endeavours to encourage him; I represented to him how pernicious any delay might be, and how very little was now wanting to the complete success of our enterprise. Non posso, tremo dalla paura,' was the only answer I could get from the frightened fool. At that moment came into my head one of those happy inspirations which are peculiar to us Southlanders, who are less believing than superstitious, and I cried out—' Madonna cara ajutaci!' sinking reverently on my knees, and turning to my fearful friend, I said to him— 'Vieni qua, facciamo una preghiera alla Madonna Santissima.' In a moment we were both before the grating of the high altar, and said five Aves and five Paternosters. It was not long before the Madonna merited the faith we placed in her. Fresh confidence streamed into Anto's sunken heart, new power into his tottering limbs. Comforted and strengthened, he rose from the floor, and before the first streaks of day lighted the topmost pinnacles of the spoliated church, we had safely reached my apartments, and placed the rich result of our midnight expedition in security.

"The broken window, and a few dropped scudi on the pavement, which had escaped out of Anto's bag, first awoke the attention of the church-keepers; but not the slightest suspicion fell on me, and as, when I was told of it, I answered jesuitically, that whoever had done it must have had a clever head, nobody thought that the clever head was actually present.

"Thus I became, if not rich, still in possession of a fair capital, which would allow me to extend my business, and to enter on several little speculations. In our country there are but two ways of rapid progress—the priesthood and the monopoly. The monopolies are monopolised by the Torlonias, the Grazolis, the Ferrajuolis, and many other parvenus of the Roman aristocracy, thanks to their titles of dukes and princes, their honours and their jewels. With the intention of following so encouraging an example, I began to buy up in the neighbouring districts certain products, in order that I might afterwards re-sell them at high rates, by getting them all in my power. If a man can afford the outlay, and the goods are such as will not spoil, the undertaking is safe, and the profit will not fail.

"One year had passed away without my secret plans and my increasing wealth exciting any suspicion amongst the still active inquirers into the church robbery. My speculations succeeded so well that I had now many hundred scudi at my disposal, besides the greater part of the two thousand which were my share of the spoil, and which lay concealed, in bags of two hundred, in a barn at some distance from my house, and in a number of sacks of Turkish wheat.

" Besides Anto, who, by means of his small participation in the booty, had much risen in the world, and was engaged to the handsome daughter of a landholder of Osimo, I employed in my business the help of a certain hunchback, whose diminutive figure secured him the nickname of ' L'uomicciuolo,' and whom I found extremely useful. Still, when I entrusted to him considerable sums of money, in the buying and selling of different goods, I never confided to him the secret of riches, because his disgusting deformity, his fire-red, ragged hair, his slouching gait, and the false leer of his grey eyes, which never looked you fairly in the face, inspired me with an irresistible mistrust in my otherwise apparently faithful servant.

" Anto's wedding was fixed for the following morning, and gave me a good deal to do. I gave the uomicciuolo a hundred scudi, with which he was to go to Recanati and buy corn, while I took the way to Osimo to fetch some document that was needed at the marriage.

" I had walked but a very short way beyond the foot of the hill, when it struck me suddenly how imprudent I had been in putting so large a sum in this man's power. I went on my lonely way, making myself more and more miserable at this thought. My uneasiness increased every moment, and at last put me into a kind of dreamy, visionary condition. I thought that I saw the Madonna before me in all her celestial glory, and that I heard her voice pronounce these words:—' Figlio mio caro, ritorna a Loreto e riprendi la tua caparra.' The ground seemed to burn under My dear son, return to Loreto, and take back your money.
my feet. I ran back to the house of the uomicciuolo; but all the answer I got was from his sister, who told me he had gone to mass. ' That is not true,' said I; ' the bell was ringing the people out as I came away;' and I ran like a madman on to the road, asking every one I met, if they had seen the hunchback. At length I heard that he had been seen going towards Recanati. I quietly followed out this clue, and, having found him, I regained my senses, and it was easy for me to tell him I had altered my mind as to the purchase I had bid him to make, and that he should give me back the money I had entrusted to his care.

" The ceremony of Anto's marriage, the welcoming and the refreshing of the concourse of friends and acquaintance there assembled, quite effaced from my mind all traces of my late vision, and, with a light heart, I gave myself up to the gaiety of the feast. Those who had not arrived already the night before, made their early appearance in the morning, and before sunrise the roads were filled with gaily dressed groups, clad in the picturesque costume of the still unsophisticated country.

"How delightfully smiled that bright May morning on the chatting troops of women and girls, who in their scarlet holiday dresses, which never fail at these festivities, and sitting easily on their little horses or asses, approached the open and gaily adorned porch of the church! On their heads fluttered the snow-white cloth with its embroidered border, shading two brilliant eyes, from which many a searching love glance penetrated to the heart. A rich coral necklace and heavy gold earrings you may be sure were not wanting. Then might be seen, with white stockings and black knee breeches, and cloth giacchetta, and with the round flowerbedecked felt hat, the fathers, and the brothers, and the husbands of the female riders.

" The marriage was over. Following immediately after the young pair—for I was the bridesman, and deep in pleasant converse with one of my neighbours—I was in the act of joining the procession which every wedding train makes through the town before the guests assemble round the well-covered table, when suddenly a Maresciallo di Carabinieri appeared among the crowd, and, making his way to me, requested me to accompany him for a moment!

" As all the town knew that my father was a counsellor, a perito della comune, it was supposed that he required my assistance in some shape or other; and, therefore, the circumstance excited no surprise. Smiling, I left the train, with a promise to return as soon as possible. Adverse fate, however, had decided otherwise. How shall I find words, Signora, to describe my feelings, when I remarked that the carabiniere, instead of conducting me to my father, turned down the street that led to the Gendarmeria, to deliver me up to the magistrates? How shall I find words to tell you to what a point my agitation was increased, when, after the examination that then took place, T found myself incarcerated in a fearful dungeon, into whose dark vault no ray of light ever entered? I fell to the ground like a dead man. I had no sensation, but that large drops of sweat were falling from my agonised forehead, to mingle with the wet earth of my prison.

"The happiness of my life was quenched for ever at that dreadful moment! From a station of honour and respectability, I was at once plunged into the condition of the lowest criminal, only, perhaps, to be released in order to mount the scaffold, or be conducted to the galleys. For three long months I lay there without the least intimation as to my ultimate fete—without the smallest intercourse with the outward world!

" But, honoured lady, instead of paining you with the recital of my sufferings, or the many sad thoughts which occupied my mind during that anxious time, I will rather proceed to tell you, in as few words as I can, to what it was that I owed my unexpected arrest.

" Although I had followed the first warning advice of the Madonna with all due faith, and had recovered from the hunchback the 100 scudi I had intrusted to him, I was not quite quick enough, for he had already helped himself to a piece of gold out of the bag, which, as he was obtaining change for it from a shopkeeper, attracted attention by its foreign appearance. It was a Russian coin, which it was to be supposed some Russian tourist or pilgrim, during his stay at Loreto, must have offered to the Madonna.

" To a sharp-sighted priest who happened to be in the shop at the time, a suspicion of this sort must have occurred, for he begged to have it, and took it to the bureau of the sacristy, where he talked the matter over with others of his colleagues, and half-an-hour afterwards the uomicciuolo was brought up before the Delegate Monsignore Zelli, and subjected to a strict examination.

" In the presence of so high a personage, and from the suddenness of the call, the hunchback was so frightened that he told everything without reserve. He told them not only from whom he had received the piece, but related so much about me and my affairs, that their suspicions could not but be awakened. They recommended to him entire silence, and with a threat that the first word he should speak about it should inevitably cause his arrest, they allowed him to go for the present.

" It is, however, doubtful whether the evidence they had now obtained would have been sufficient to convict me as the long-sought church robber, had not another circumstance transpired which confirmed it. My wife, who, in this affair and all others in which I had been concerned, had been the most faithful of assistants, was, notwithstanding all her good qualities, not free from an inconceivable weakness which seems to characterize the whole sex. I must confess that my beautiful Vittoria, in common with most women, had a foolish passion for old and new linen, and to her niggardliness in this respect I must attribute, as the Signora will soon see, all my misfortune. As soon as I and Anto had brought home the money, I enjoined my wife to pack it in several smaller bags, and to make them herself out of new linen. You can,' said I, ' make use of the piece which old Agnese left us in pledge, and which most likely is not yet redeemed. The bags in which the money now is, must be immediately afterwards burned, as the seal and stamp of the Santa Casa are upon them.'

" The silly Vittoria did not follow my orders, but, either from superstition or avarice, she was withheld from burning the sacred bags; in short, she thought she was sufficiently following my orders by taking off all the sealing wax, and making seven smaller bags out of the two large ones. How deeply must she have repented of this, when, after the hunchback's examination, the police entered the house, and by carefully searching over the whole premises, at last discovered the bags beneath the wheat sacks, with the unmistakeable and indelible stamp upon them, which at once condemned me as the guilty party!

" As it surprised even the police, and indeed appeared incredible, that so respectable a man as Vincenzo the Doctor should be guilty of such a crime against the Madonna, every one else at once pronounced in my favour, and not half the evidence was produced that might have been. The weaver and a washer-woman of the Santa Casa answered when questioned, the former, Ho tessuto questa tela, ma ne ho tessuto tante;' and the latter, 'Tela, uva, ove, e denari non si riconoscono piu.' f

" Meantime, I pined in my prison, in the anticipation of what might be my fate. As a galley-slave, condemned for life, must wear the heavy chains to his latest breath, so should I bear the consequence of this act, arising more from youthful thoughtlessness than anything else, to the grave itself.

" The inquiry took the usual course. Everything made against me, and deprived me of every gleam of hope. I pleaded every excuse which had proved available in former processes; but the godless robbery which the law designated as ' furto magno,' and ' furto sacrilego,' could not be thus evaded. Everything was tried, but without effect, and l was condemned I may have woven this linen, but I have woven so much more also, f Linen, grapes, eggs, and coin, are difficult to identify.

to death! As such a judgment, however, is never executed except in cases of murder, my sentence was commuted to imprisonment for life!

" Two long years I lay in the dark

dungeon of Loreto, and then was taken to Osimo, where I shared my imprisonment with many others, a circumstance which at least gave me the prospect of a possibility of escape. We soon agreed together to make the attempt, and consulted on the ways and means. A broken iron collar, which doubtless had encircled the throat of many of my predecessors, and which we found fixed to the wall, proved of the greatest use to us. We contrived to straighten it, and formed it into a kind of tool, with which we undertook the tedious task of boring through the wall.

" Months elapsed before any satisfactory result was obtained; but we attained our end at last, without our gaoler having any suspicion; and triumphantly beat our hearts at the thought that in a few hours the golden joys of freedom would reward our unceasing labour! A number of female convicts of the lowest grade were confined in a cell beneath our walls, and as it was to be feared that the fall of any of the stonework would cause them to announce their fears by their cries, we cast lots for the rotation in which we should leap down, seeing that the last would thus run so much greater risk of being prevented from escaping.

" Fortune favoured me, and I drew the lot which entitled me to the first chance. Excitement and courage often serve men like arms and shields. Although a leap of twenty feet was before me, I reached the bottom in safety. Three others took the leap with similar success, but scarcely could the fourth follow, when a fearful cry issued from the building beneath our cell. Of course, each now thought only of his own security, and with the celerity which the danger of the moment required, we rushed from the neighbourhood of the prison.

" For fear of being betrayed by our prison dress, we had nothing on but our under clothing, and if ever I suffered from cold, it was on that memorable January night, when, half naked and barefooted, we ran across the snow-covered fields!

" Before break of day we reached my father's house. My aged mother's heart must have warned her that her son was approaching, for hardly had the dogs announced our arrival, than she appeared at a window in the upper story. At the first whispered word she recognised my voice, and hastened down to open the door to me, while my father forbade her to offer me shelter and protection. However, through an open window she gave us food and wine and clothes. ' I have no capottina to give you, my son,' she said, but go to our neighbour, old Giacomo, and he will surely furnish you with an old coat.'

" It was now full daylight, and high time for us to proceed in our further flight. I followed my mother's advice, and soon obtained a capottina from Giacomo. I returned to our house, where I left my companions warming themselves at a fine fire; but what was my grief when, instead of them, I was met by a troop of carabinieri, who at once took me prisoner again!

" My flight having made me doubly guilty, I was treated with double severity, and although my former sufferings were hard to bear, my present and future state was still more wretched. I was loaded with chains, and put into the ' Segreta,' the worst of all the dungeons, as perhaps the Signora may have heard. Not the faintest glimmer of daylight or lamp

E light ever broke through the darkness of this dreadful cell, where I felt myself condemned to endless night and hopeless solitude! The chains which were fixed to my feet weighed upwards of 100 pounds.

" After having been seventeen months in the Segreta, it seemed to me that a longer continuance of such a martyrdom must destroy cither my reason or my health, or both; and I swore to myself, that either dead or alive I would be released! and therefore resolved neither to eat nor drink, bit or sup, until they brought me before the court. My gaoler observed that I neither eat nor drank any of the food he left with me daily, and began to fear that some morning he might find me a corpse; and as I answered his repeated injunctions to take food, only by saying that I would not do so till I had been before the judges, I one evening found that my perseverance had been successful, and I received a visit from the governor. As I had no hope of actual release, my prayer to this high dignitary went no further than that I should be sent to the galleys, and allowed to work with the other slaves, at least, in the open air.

" I was accordingly sent to Ancona, and attached to one of these bands. In consequence of my former situation and my heavy fate, and the patience with which I bore it, I began to be looked upon by the inhabitants of Ancona with much curiosity, and I found also that my renown had preceded my arrival. No popish legate could be more enthusiastically received; but this being thought a dangerous precedent, I was at once removed to Civita Vecchia.

" My renown, however, had travelled thither also; and on my arrival at that (then) insignificant town, I was welcomed with a band of music and the acclamations of the townsfolk.

" Although I underwent the usual lot of all galley slaves in Civita Vecchia, and, except during working hours, I was chained, the high esteem in which I was held by my companions decreased the hardness of my fate; and it was doubtless the lightest that ever was accorded to one in my case. With the lower herds of criminals I took no part, but I made many friendships with robber chiefs and other celebrities, who, by personal courage, temerity, and cunning, on the Pontine Marshes, the Sabine Hills, or the Apennines, had acquired distinction. Under many a rough form I found a noble heart, capable of any generous sacrifice. I will only instance Gasperone, who refused the pardon offered him by Pius IX. because it was not extended to his comrades also.

" Before long, I was appointed ' Camerlengo' of the whole band; and so inherent is pride and lust of office in every human breast, that even this imaginary superiority over a band of malefactors was some consolation for the loss of freedom, especially when I received the news of my mother's death, and the early departure also of my poor Vittoria, and that my father had disinherited me.

" A dangerous illness was the consequence of these tidings; and I was then allowed more freedom. I was permitted to walk for two hours, and afterwards to learn the business of a basket-maker.

" The accession of Pius IX. opened the doors of many prisons, and on my fate also had its effect. After a seven years' servitude at Civita Vecchia, I was brought to Porto d'Anzo, and, after two years more, was removed, as pardoned, to my native town.

" My behaviour there soon won the confidence of the police, under whose supervisal I still was. The ceremony of putting me into security every night was gradually relaxed. From compassion at my loss of relations, or some other reason, I was gifted with a small annual pension, on which, eked out by the few bajocchi which I earned at my trade of basket-making, I contrived to live with some approach to enjoyment of life.

" My daughters, famed for their beauty, were married in the Romagna. The farm on which I had passed the careless hours of childhood and the bright years of youth had become the property of strangers. It is not a little flattering to me to have excited so much sensation by my hard fate and my sufferings, and I feel honoured at finding a title attached to my name.

" At every step, and as often as I appear in the streets, I hear the remark, ' There goes the great philosopher!' passing from mouth to mouth; and I am persuaded that my celebrity will live in the memory of the. world, like that of a Napoleon. But, firm as my belief still remains that it is wicked to waste costly gifts upon a lifeless image, I confess I could not recommend others to follow my example; but rather, I would advise all my countrymen who seek for reputation, honour, and riches, to aim at the Episcopal ring and the Cardinal's hat, which are the only and undoubted means in this country to arrive, by a safe road, at the fount of all worldly good fortune." CHAPTER IV.

;FROM LORETO TO FLORENCE.

Very early next morning I left Loreto, not by the high road that takes you by way of Osimo to Ancona, but by the nearer, though more hilly, route through Camerano and Crocelle.

" I was much concerned, Signora," said Giuseppe, as soon as we got out of the town, " to hear that you had sent for the Doctor yesterday. I hope the Signora is not unwell? " said I to the waiter, with some apprehension. " Not at all," said he; "the Doctor who is with your lady is no medical man, but a great philosopher, who can tell her many strange things."

I gave Giuseppe a full account of my interview with the pseudo Doctor, and we then proceeded on our way.

The Camerano road runs between the seashore and the post road, so that I only saw Osimo in the distance. He who rides from Loreto to Ancona must arm himself with patience, for the country is very deceptive to the eye.

The land bordering on the coast is cut up by little hills, low enough to be overlooked at a distance, but high enough every moment to exclude the view. The consequence is, that with so much up and down work, you are always farther from any particular part than appears to be the case; and even when this comes to an end, and you reach the gates of Ancona, it takes a long time to pass all the fortifications, and to thread the thronged streets, before you arrive at the Hotel della Pace, whose cool rooms and capital arrangements are very welcome after a twenty-one miles march.

Ancona is an interesting little town, possessing its classical as well as its historical value; but the ever increasing industry which obtains here, under the privilege of a free port, the continual departures and arrivals of steamers, which keep up a constant communication with Trieste, Malta, and the ports of the East, throw, for the moment, its classical memories into the background. I had been there before, and had no need to remain very long at present. Many years ago, when bound on a visit to the Ionian Islands, I had time and leisure to see all that was to be seen. But I was still glad to employ the time of my mid-

day rest in walking through the streets of the new part of the town. Juvenal writes of Ancona, and the Emperor Trajan embellished it with several fine marble buildings. The popes did the same, and in many historical occurrences it has played a prominent part. It may also boast of having produced several men of note, and has been rich in beautiful women; and of these one, the so-called "Heroine of Ancona," obtained an undying renown by having, when the town was besieged in 1173 by the Ghibelines, during a dreadful famine, denied the nourishment of the breast to her own child, in order to give it to a fainting warrior, who, as it is said, strengthened by the reviving stream, grasped his weapon with a renewed energy, to risk his life for his country's good.

Occupied with these recollections, I directed my steps to the pier, where the Trajan's Arch, which crowns its ancient part, and the Pope's Arch, which crowns the modern half, have caused no little criticism, but, nevertheless, it is a building worthy of much admiration. I was obliged, however, to hasten on, for my riding habit caused rather too much observation.

On my return, I asked the landlord if ladies never rode in Ancona? Very seldom in the town, he told me; and a Roman lady, Emma Gagiotti, was the only one he could recollect passing through the streets " en Amazone." From further inquiries, I found that this Corinne of the nineteenth century, who about ten years ago was the object of universal admiration for her beauty, her talents in music, painting, and languages, was now living here in retirement with her family. The marriage which she foolishly contracted with a rich Englishman proved unhappy.

To my mind, the pleasantest part of an equestrian tour is when one turns one's back on a large town, and again comes to the open country and pure air. Ballerino must have been of the same opinion, for he sprang through the last gate and over the last drawbridge, not in the least regarding the police there stationed; and, indeed, I did not restrain him, as I always left all passport arrangements to Giuseppe. A morose douanier was much offended at this, and with the malicious question " whether we had anything contraband upon us," he seized my bridle rein before I could prevent it. Such a question to those whom their passport showed to have ridden *already* 200 miles on horseback, and to have much more before them, seemed to me so scandalous that I gave him no answer, but urged my horse forward. " But what have you got in that basket?" said he, pointing to the puppy's hanging cradle. " Look for yourself," said I, " and if it is subject to duty, let me know what I have to pay." With a triumphant smile, as if expecting to find something of importance, the douanier went to the basket and woke up the little puppy into a snarl and a bark, which caused a general laugh, and the characteristic remark, that if I had opened my basket at first there would have been no need to look at my passport, as nobody but "una Bignora Inglese " would ever carry a dog hanging at her saddle!

Anything so uniform as the twenty miles from Ancona to Sinigaglia is not easy to find. On one side is the level sea, and on the other a landscape as level.

Unfavourably as this monotony contrasted with the fair scene of the previous day, it still had a charm for me; for the monotony of the sea, as well as of the desert, is but seeming. At the sea-side there is really no sameness—nature there is in a constant change—colours, light and shade, are continually altering, and this is the more visible, because there are no land-like forms to break the outline and attract the attention.

Then, what animation is given by the gigantic steamer and the three-masted ship, picturesquely rigged feluccas and fishing craft—to such a sea as the Adriatic, to whose waters the cloudless blue of the bright sky imparts its colour! Sometimes we exchanged the hard chalky white road for the soft sea-sand, and the foam of the gentle waves refreshed the feet of our horses; and there blew such a reviving breeze, that almost before we were aware of it we had passed the station of Ansicata, and an hour later we reached our night quarters at Sinigaglia.

One of the chief interests attached to this town, the successor of the ancient " Sena Gallica," is the widely-renowned yearly market of Santa Maria Madalena, which for more than six centuries has been held here, and is so held, up to this present time, with all its original usages, and on its original site. Everything needful or desirable, from the costly clothing of the rich and noble to the commonest article in use amongst the peasants and labourers, is to be met with at this fair. Merchants from Venice, Geneva, Trieste, France and Germany, and the Levant, bring hither their different commodities; not in small bundles, to tempt the easily tempted traveller, but in bales and chests, to supply the inland trade of the whole country. Every house is turned into a shop, and the whole town into a bazaar. There is hardly a European language which may not be heard in the crowded emporium, and every dialect of the Italian provinces meets the ear.

If I did not find the town in the fever of this animated time—for it takes place on the 20th July, lasting till the 8th August—I found it in scarcely a less agitation.

It was celebrating the arrival of the Pope, for his first visit to his native place since his accession to the throne. His Holiness had arrived the evening before, and at the moment when we, dusty, exhausted, and thirsty, rode into the town, the Pope was making a gala tour round it, with a splendid train, and every honour that could be heaped upon him. This was very unfortunate for our tired horses, for, of course, every avenue was stopped, and we could scarcely meet with any one sufficiently unoccupied to show us by what back-way we could gain the " Formica," the only hotel in Sinigaglia! After a long trial of patience, many questions, and repeated mistakes, we at length caught sight of the " Formica;" and as at this point the bustle was at the highest, Giuseppe left his horse to my care, and hastened up to the inn to see if he could secure us a lodging. I saw him, with disappointed mien, going from house to house, and from stable to stable, from public-house to public-house, till he was almost knocked up. At length a gendarme told me I must retire into a bye-street with my horses, as the papal procession was approaching! Of course I was obliged to follow his directions, and thus I saw very little of the sight, as I was placed behind some thick trees, and the noise alone told me that it was passing by. The Corese soon afterwards found me in my hiding-place, and brought me tidings that we should fare very badly as to our night quarters. The noble Ballerino and his brave comrade would have to make common companionship with about thirty miserable horses, mules, asses, and goats; while I was to have a bed in the house of a good-natured farmer's wife. Without any attention to the calls of hunger and thirst, I changed my habit quickly for a less remarkable dress, and hastened to deliver two letters of introduction which his

Excellency Monsignore B had given me to his brothers. Of course on such a day as this I could hardly expect to find them—for the one being " Gonfaloniere," and the other " Sindaco," they must be in attendance with the Pope. Without the aid of Giuseppe's strong arm, I should never have got through the crowd.

It is impossible to deny that the Italians have great taste and aptitude in arranging these festivities. During my long residence in the South, I had frequently had opportunities of seeing and admiring this innate genius for art, but the Sinigaglians surpassed all my former experiences, whether in the Tuscan, Roman, or Neapolitan Governments; and when I say that the whole town seemed metamorphosed into a universal ball-room, I give the reader but a faint idea of the dazzling effect of the reality.

The air was loaded with the scent of myrtles and laurel boughs, which formed a soft carpet over the sand-strewn streets. From house to house, on each side of the way, were stretched tapestry awnings. Red, green, white, blue, and yellow lamps vied in colour and brightness with flowering plants. Old and young, full-dressed women, laughing maidens, and wanton children, composed the crowd, while they greeted each other as acquaintances and friends, met and passed, or expressed their pleasure at the beauty of the spectacle. Here, came a chorus of men, singing " La bandiera bianca;" there, an orchestre performed favourite opera airs. Here, a company were refreshing themselves with ices and " sorbetti;" there, a rising fire-balloon occupied the spectators. Here, a band of country folk; there, a posse of sailors attracted attention by the execution of their characteristic dances. Wherever you came were highly decorated arches, beautiful drapery hanging from every window; and at last, when the sun had sunk to rest in the west, and twilight fell upon the scene, thousands upon thousands of lamps suddenly illuminated the streets—lamps of all forms and all sizes, and some decorated with allegorical painting, armorial bearings, and sententious mottoes. The front of the palace appropriated to the Pope was a complete sea of fire. The little marine of Sinigaglia also lent its aid to the brilliancy of the *fete.* In the harbour which stretches into the town, from ship to ship, felucca to felucca, bark to bark, were stretched ropes with flags and lamps, while an appointed squadron did its part in the show by several salvos of artillery.

Without attempting to fathom, without daring to measure, how much of this ovation was to be attributed to the papal dignity, or to the burger of Sinigaglia, Mastai-Ferretti, personally, —whether flattered self-love or pleasing his fellow-citizens were the chief motives to the display—I wandered about until the forty and odd miles I had ridden that day began to tell upon my strength, and, as the next day I proposed to have another long march, I thought it prudent to seek the " Formica" again, especially as the festivities had assumed a rather too bacchanalian character.

I was not a little surprised to find the Gonfalionere and Sindaco waiting at my hotel for me, these gentlemen having, when their duty was over, found the letters I had delivered at their houses, and hurried off to pay me a visit. In this kind attention I recognized the same spirit of hospitality which had induced their brother for so many years to favour me with so many civilities. They pressed me to defer my departure, and to accompany them to some of the festivities of the evening; but, for many reasons, I declined their friendly eagerness, and confined myself to a few minutes' pleasant conversation with them. They expressed much regret that I had not arrived the previous evening, that I might have witnessed the Pope's reception—not on account of the splendid ceremonies of the day, but because, they said, it had been really interesting to see the sensibility, the humble and grateful spirit which Pius IX. had exhibited on the occasion. Deeply impressed at his return to his birthplace, and overwhelmed with the feelings it called forth, he could scarcely repress them when he saw the enthusiasm of his fellow-townsmen, and tears dimmed his eye as he gave them a silent blessing. When they brought him to the palace prepared for his reception, he declined to enter it, and spent the first night in the simple chamber of the burger-house where he drew his first breath. The time which was not occupied with the ceremony of the day, he spent in visiting some of the friends of his youth and persons of all classes with whom he had any acquaintance during the years of his private life, and in relieving the necessities of the poor and miserable.

I may here be permitted to repeat an anecdote, which I have on the authority of the person most interested in it, and which may be amusing to the reader, not only for the pretty *bon-mot* it contains, but because it is a confirmation of the opinion the two brothers gave of the Holy Father.

Among the young men to whom the Count Mastai-Ferretti was attached during his student years at Volterra,was a Piedmontese Dominican monk, of the name of Gaude. With this man he formed a close friendship, until his return to Rome took him away from the place, and interrupted his intercourse with the monk. The Count, meanwhile, took orders, became a priest, and undertook, in 1823, a mission to Chili. After his return he devoted himself to the cause of the poor, and was made President of the Provident Institution at San Michele. When the Pope Leo XII. subsequently made him Archbishop of Spoleto, and he was thus in a situation to offer his former curate a remunerative employment near himself, he invited him to visit him. But a still higher rank again called him away, and, being raised to the Archbishopric of Imola, in 1833, by Gregory XVI., his favourite Gaude and he were again divided. The archbishopric was followed by a Cardinal's hat, and this by the papal tiara. Thirteen years had passed by, during which time Gaude had heard nothing direct from his patron; but during this long term nothing made Pius forget his old favourite, and he had not been long elected the successor of Gregory XVI. when he sent for Gaude, and appointed him Director of the " Seminario Pio."

This honourable situation Gaude had filled for nine years, not dreaming that Pius IX. had any further intentions towards him, until one day His Holiness paid a visit to the Seminario, and after inspecting it, and signifying his satisfaction with the Director, he expressed a wish to speak further with him, and desired him to take a chair beside him. Although it was not allowed to any one below the rank of Cardinal to sit in the presence of the Pope, the Director was not surprised, because from his youth he had suffered from a lameness which forbade him to stand for any length of time. Still, as he hesitated respectfully, the Pope with his own hand reached him a chair, and with that affability which had won so many hearts, he placed his hand on his friend's shoulder, and said to him, "Gaude, Gaude et laetare, presto si fa Cardinale."

With this pleasant play upon words was the unassuming but meritorious Dominican most unexpectedly raised to an honour which many an ambitious man has doubtless spent his life in endeavouring to attain, and which would have been too costly to the poor monk himself, had not the Pope at the same time defrayed all the expenses attending his elevation.

Some months after this occurrence, when the new cardinal had his first reception in his palace of " Cardinale Vicario," I remember to have been there myself; and as I saw the jewelled Italian princesses and the crowd of curious foreigners passing through the beautiful rooms, I did not expect that the highly honoured but humble Dominican would one day relate to me, in a friendly circle, the story of his rapid elevation.... But my reader must now take leave of the festivities of Sinigaglia, and follow the solitary rider once more.

At the mouth of the Metauro and across a plain, nearly twenty miles from Sinigaglia, lies Fano, the " Fanum Fortunse " of the ancients, which belonged to the cities of Pentapolis. Here I had intended to rest, but a part of the Pope's convoy was there, and all entertainment for man and beast was already monopolized. In order to avoid this company, I skirted the town, and was thus deprived of the sight of several objects worthy of inspection, particularly a marble triumphal arch raised by Augustus, and some fine pictures in the church of Fano.

This town, like most others in the Romagna, can boast of having furnished an occupant of the papal chair, being the birthplace of Clement VIII. But its greatest honour consists in having established the first printing press in which the Arabic letters were used, and that at the cost of Pope Julius II.

After a hasty meal at La Cattolica, I rode on as far as Rimini; a name with which every one must be familiar, as being the scene of the misfortune of the beautiful daughter of Guido da Polenta.

Is it to be wondered at that her love, her fault, and her punishment, arose from the perusal of that touching episode in Dante's " Divina Commedia," when one thinks that the great poet was a beloved friend and *protege* of the proud Lord of Ravenna, and that he had seen Francisca, glowing with innocence and beauty, rise from childhood to girlhood, from girlhood to womanhood, under her father's roof? He wrote that pathetic tale in the same house in which Francisca was born, and where he found an asylum during the last ten years of his exile.

Of Francisca's house there is nothing now to be seen; it has become amalgamated with the

Palazzo Ruffi, or perhaps the latter has been built where the former once stood. I strolled on to the market-place, where I saw a stone with the following inscription—

C. Cffisar Diet. Bubicone superato Civili Bat.
Commilit suos hie in foro Ar. adlocut.

From this stone Caesar had addressed his soldiers. The die was cast; the Rubicon passed; and the word was " Forward."

Only a few hundred years later, and St. Antonio held a discourse here also; but as there was a scarcity of human auditors, he addressed the fishes!

It requires to be an old traveller in Italy, or at least one who loves to linger over classic ground, to feel all the true pleasure that is to be enjoyed in visiting certain localities and towns whose historical and poetical interest awakens again our youthful sympathies; but in order to know how inexhaustible a source of this pleasure Italy is, he must visit it on horseback, that he may find, as he will at almost every step, something worth his notice. If the summer months had not been too short, if I had not other duties which called me elsewhere, I should have rejoiced to have devoted much longer time to my present tour. I mention this only to excuse my apparent neglect of much that is worthy of observation, and at the same time to make those who follow my steps aware, that if they will do it as it ought to be done, they must have an unlimited credit on the Bank of Time.

I left Rimini very unwillingly, but still more did I regret that I must now abandon Adria and enter the inland road to Forli, without paying a visit to the lovely environs of Ravenna, that chief city of the Western Empire, the seat of the Gothic and Longobardic kings, the metropolis of the Greek exarchs! Rome-like, she mourns in utter loneliness over her bygone celebrity; and yet how exalted, how grand, how rich in their fallen state are both! In Ravenna's classic "Pineto," Dante loved to dream and to breathe its inspiration into his noble poetry. Boccaccio's tale " Nastagio degli Onesti," goes on in that wood. Dryden's muse has done homage to it; and Byron has not left it unsung. Here grew the mighty trunks out of whose planks Rome built her stately galleys; and from these pines were selected the lofty masts which bore the banners of Venice. At Ravenna is the sepulchre of Dante, at the door of which Chateaubriand, bareheaded, knelt before he entered; and on the tomb within Byron placed a copy of his works as an offering! At this sanctuary Alfieri wrote one of his finest sonnets, while reverently bending to the earth:

" O gran padre Alighier, se dal ciol miri
Me tuo discepol non indegno Btarmi,
Dal cor traendo profondi sospiri
Prostrato innanzi a 'tuoi funerei marmi. "
#

The country between Rimini and Cesena is chiefly interesting from Caesar's passage of the Rubicon. Besides a stream of considerable breadth, over which there is an ancient bridge, and which to this day bears the name of " II Rubicone," there are three other small rivers which run into the Adriatic, and which contend with the real Rubicon in forming the boundary of Cis-Alpine Gaul. These are the Savignano, the Pisatello, and the Rugone. A clear proof that p that the above mentioned river is the true Rubicon, is the circumstance that the country people, who have no archseologic or geographic theory to support, have always given it that appellation.

My approach to Cesena is among the most enjoyable moments of my tour, and will never depart from my memory. Bathed in a gorgeous sunset the landscape lay before me, as I began the ascent of the hill, on whose summit the town stands. To the right, in the far distance, glances the sea, dotted with vessels, and the coast now clothed in spring-like verdure, while the picturesque town, and a boldly rising height crowned with a church and monastery, bound my view to the left. It was in this fine church of " Santa Maria del Monte" that Pius VII. took his vows as Bendictine monk, to enter as Padre Chiaramonte in the adjoining monastery. Sweet smells added to the beauty of the picture. Trains of peasants going home from their labour; groups of mowers with their scythes, shortening their way with song and dance; grave shepherds conducting their flocks over the plain; herdsmen and women driving their cattle to water, enlivened the scene so pleasantly, that I often checked Ballerino in his quick paces, to enjoy it the longer. Nor were more elegant figures wanting, and the richer inhabitants of Cesena, on foot or in carriages, had come out to take the air.

Two " elegants " in a calessiuo drawn by a handsome horse seemed to be admiring my horses. They had driven by my side for about a mile, when, with a respectful bow, they asked me if I had come from Sinigaglia, and if I could give them any account of the Pope's arrival there? I told them all I knew, and this induced a conversation, from which I discovered that they were of one of the best families in Cesena, and heard to my regret, that I should have the greatest difficulty in obtaining a lodging in the already overfilled town, where not only every inn, but every private house was crowded with visitors, and that many would have to pass the night " a la belle etoile." Before they left me, one of them presented me with the most delicate bouquet I ever saw, consisting of freshly gathered damask roses, of the choicest kind, which he had brought from his villa.

We did not find Cesena so gaily decorated as Sinigaglia was, but the inhabitants had taken the same fever; and as the Pope's arrival was being delayed, you saw impatience, mistrust, and restlessness in every feature. A festive crowd thronged the streets, and it was no trifle to make our way through them. Every one seemed to have other things to do than to attend to me, and a moment of doubt overcame me, as I saw the clear impossibility of obtaining a room. Still it was as impossible to go on, for I, as well as my horses, were completely tired.

Giuseppe jumped from his saddle in order to make an attempt to find some sort of a shelter, and returned to say that he had seen a kind of a " grotto," in which he thought the horses might be housed, provided I was content with a little room, which the woman to whom it belonged had offered him. Of course this offer was not refused. The good woman appeared, and after walking through a labyrinth of alleys, she entered a little earth-built hut, where I had to climb a ladder, which brought me into a hot chamber. It was broad, but very low, and with its many trap-doors, sliding cupboards and exits, had a very *coupe gorge* appearance. Had not Gil Bias' adventures occurred in Spain, I should have taken it for one of those "loci casdibus infames " he so graphically describes. All that remained for me, however, was to secure it, such as it was, and to ascertain that there were to be no occupants of the second bed which the room contained. " Only two or three men had applied for it," said the woman. " My good friend," said I, " that will never do—I will pay you as much as if you had let both beds, but I must be aforee." "That will cost you something," said she, with undisguised astonishment at my luxurious tendencies. "And how can it be untenanted, when the door cannot be closed? "

However, I insisted that I must have my way, and only begged to know what I must pay for it. " Well, I can't take less than two paoli," was the result; and of course I was obliged to agree to her terms, provided she would supply me with some things that were necessary. However, except a lamp and a jug of water, I got nothing of what I required, nor did I see the woman again. I was ignorant, also, where my servant and the horses were, and thus I saw myself entirely cut off from the world, and condemned to this suspicious looking chamber, which I dared not leave, for fear of having all my property stolen.

I have purposely been so particular in describing my lodging at Cesena, in order to give the reader some notion of the primitive condition in which parts of Italy still slumber, where the Pioneer-English traveller has not yet found his way, and to make any who are disposed to try it, aware what they have to expect. In hoping to get any sleep in this comfortless room, I was reckoning entirely on the great fatigue I had undergone. Still I could not lay me down without, attended by my dog and armed with my lamp, first having a close inspection of every corner of the place, and ascertaining to what each door led. At one of them my dog was sniffing and whining, and I could not help looking farther; and my alarm was not small, when I saw an immense shepherd's dog, and, farther on, a number of snoring men and women on a row of miserable beds. With the speed of lightning I shut the door again. They might be harmless people enough, but I should have remained very uneasy if I had not at that moment discovered a strong bar, and, fixing it across the door, I wished my neighbours good night, and secured myself from any friendly or unfriendly intercourse with them.

Fortunately, my rest was undisturbed, and, notwithstanding my surroundings, I slept well and long, and was only awakened next morning by the well known knock of Giuseppe at my door.

We had not long left the city when the sight of the river Savio reminded me that, if a reckless Robert von Genf had written the name of Cesena in history with letters of blood, a Dante had immortalized it by his kind remembrance, speaking of it as

" Quella, a cui il Savio bagna il fianeo,
Cosi com 'ella siede tra il piano e il monte
Tra tirannia si vive e stato franco."

A capital road, which has been formed on the foundation of the ancient " Via Emilia," leads through a fruitful plain to Forli; and when we had passed the Apennine mountain streams of Aria, Bevanella, Bevano, and Avusa, we arrived at the little town of Forlimpopoli, a name very little altered from the old one of Forum Popilii, which, like most places on this coast, was one of the scenes of the struggle between Murat and the Allied Powers, until at last the decisive fight at Tolentino drove him out of the Roman States. Not far from Forlimpopoli we pass the river Romo, and then reach Forli, rich in classical and mediaeval recollections.

Although not more than eighteen miles from Cesena, I determined on remaining here the rest of the day, and making it my night quarters also, seeing that our next stage over the Apennines would be a fatiguing one, and presenting very few good places for a halt.

Forli lies just at the foot of the mountains, in a fine and productive valley, watered by the Romo and the Montone, and is well worth a short visit. The antiquity of its church, a chamber in the town hall, painted by Raphael, and the handsome market-place, are all worth inspection, as well as the old ruined walls, and all possess historical value of some kind. I will only instance the heroism of Catherina Sforza. Her husband, Girolamo Riario, the nephew, or as some think him, the son of Sixtus IV., was Lord of Forli and Rimini. He had played a conspicuous part in the Pazzi conspiracy, and was, it is said, at the instigation of Lorenzo di Medici, poignarded by two of his officers, while fining in his palace at Forli. The populace dragged the body, which had been thrown from a window into the street, round the city walls; but as the insurgents, after they had seized upon his wife and children and put them into prison, demanded the key of the citadel, the commandant refused to give it up without the personal permission of Catherina Sforza. The conspirators, therefore, allowed her to pass into the city, keeping the children as pledges; but no sooner was she within the walls than she ordered them to be fired upon, and seeing them preparing to revenge themselves on her children, she mounted the wall, and cried out, " If you kill them, recollect that I have still a son in Imola, and carry another in my womb, both of whom will one day be old enough to avenge such a crime."

The people, intimidated by the courage she displayed, did not carry out their revengeful intentions. At a later period this same Catherina defended Forli against the united powers of France and the States of the Church, although, after an heroic contest, in which she disputed every inch of ground, retreating from town to town, she was at last taken prisoner, and sent to the Castle of St. Angelo. # #

At 4 o'clock the next morning we left Forli, wrapt in the stillness of night, and we had not proceeded far before I missed my beautiful greyhound, who had followed me so many hundred miles. We had passed the village of Varano, three miles from Forli, when turning round to look for her, she was nowhere to be seen. Determined to return to Forli, and take every step to recover her, I was just putting the plan into execution, when we observed the poor dog running after us, and I feel persuaded that she had escaped from some one who intended to steal her. I was resolved to be more careful in future, and to carry her in my lap over the mountains.

Precisely on this very day, when we had so long a march before us, every thing seemed to be against us. Having repassed Varano, I was long detained at Rovere by matters relating to my passport. At Terra del Sole, the Tuscan border town, I was much hindered by the curiosity of the inhabitants, on account of my mode of travelling; so that after five hours and a half we had only accomplished thirteen miles. In the Locanda del Giglio, a miserable hedge inn, where we had to rest our horses, only one kitchen, filled with tobacco smoke and drinking boors, was to be found, and I was obliged to walk out and look about the village, which lies on the Montone, just where two other small streams run into it.

It was Sunday, and I walked towards the church upon the hill, whence I could already distinguish the sound of the organ. However, in this small place, where scarcely ever a visitor is seen, my dress, and the circumstance of having travelled on horseback, produced so much sensation, that I was quickly encompassed by half the village, and could proceed neither forwards nor backwards. Not having Giuseppe with me, I had no alternative but to go back to the inn, and let myself be smoked in patience, until the horses were ready to go forward.

The road over the Apennine pass of San Godenzo was opened only a few years ago by the Tuscan Government, with the view of forming a communication between Florence, Rimini, Ravenna, and the other cities of the north western coast of the Adriatic Sea. Its construction is according to modern art, and it is excellently attended to; and it only requires that the tourists should have a hint of this, to bring a concourse of travellers to enjoy the pleasures it affords.

From Rocca San Casciano the road follows the windings of the Montone, and at the passing of the old fortified town ' Portico,' at a distance of twelve miles, is the village of San Benedetto, where the ascent of the mountains begins. As we were obliged to stop to give the horses rest, the innkeeper seemed to think we must also pass the night here, and did his best to describe to me what a night I might have if I did not! If the ' Leone d'Oro ' had been the best hotel possible, I should not have altered my plan of reaching Corbonile the same evening, as I did not wish to lose a day in my arrival at Florence, although I do not deny that it put both me and the horses to some fatigue, and I could not conscientiously advise any one to follow my example, yet the evening ride over the mountains gave me enjoyment that I would not have missed. What can be more delightful than to ride in the bright sunset of a southern clime, through the variable scene of a mountain road, where almost every foot in the ascent affords one a change of vegetation and a more distant prospect. Evergreen trees, nicely built terraces, and the soft pasture land, we had left behind us; and the cornfields, the chesnuts and the fruit trees, must give place to the oak and the beech? Here in these high and silent regions, and in this vaporous air, a panorama of wild rocks and mountain chains, such as I had never seen before, rose before my eyes. Then, everything seemed stretched at my feet, and I experienced the sensation of being at the summit of a glorious mountain! Peacefully closed in the evening upon this splendid scene. No motion, no sound, disturbed the quiet. The road which wound from one mountain wall to another, and the noiseless rising of a solitary eagle, were the only proofs we saw that this desert was ever trodden by men, or inhabited by animals. Majestic was the flight of the kingly bird, hastening to his nest, while approaching night spread her shadows around us.

The group of houses which gives the name of San Godenzo to this pass, is situated a short distance after passing the extreme ridge. The six miles which were still before us we began to look upon as a real evil, a sensible " revers de la medaille." I cannot leave unnoticed the brave endurance with which the horses had undergone so trying a journey. Notwithstanding their fatigue and the darkness, they never made a false step; and, indeed, it seemed as if, with my impatience to arrive at Carbonile, their courage and good-will increased, and they bore us along with indefatigable perseverance. With what pleasure did I at length perceive the distant light of the lonely house, where these faithful servants were to forget their fatigue! We had ridden over nearly sixty Roman miles, and the ride had brought with it so much trouble, but so much enjoyment at the same time, that I made sure of a good night's rest, even had the little inn been less comfortable than it was. Tuscan civilization was very apparent in this out of the way place; and as a proof that as yet no foreign travellers had spoiled its primitive prices, I may mention that three paoletti were the entire charge for lodging, supper, and breakfast.

A charming ride across the wooded valley of the Sieve brought us the following day to Pontassieve, a place at which the rushing mountain stream which had hitherto been our companion falls into the Arno, and the post roads from Forli and Arezzo to Florence join. Our approach to a large town soon became apparent. Farm followed farm, villa villa, and house house. I remembered the beautiful lines of Ariosto in which he speaks of the environs of Florence.

" A veder pien di tante ville i colli
Par che il terren ve le germogli come
Vermene germogliar suole e rampolli;
Se dcntra tin mur, sotto un medesmo nome
Fosser raccolti i tuoi palazzi sparsi
Non ti sarien da pareggiar due Rome."

Florence " La bella " was before me. I was at the Porta alla Croce. A few steps through the narrow streets brought me to the pleasant Lung'Arno and an hotel distinguished by Tuscan cleanliness and comfort—doubly enjoyable after such a journey.

But you, my reader, who have experienced only the pleasures of my 400 miles ride, may be ready at once for the palatial streets of the old city! Procure, then, your guide! visit the Medicean Venus, and the Madonna della Seggiola, and mount the hill of Bellosguardo, to revel in the sweet view of the Tale of Arno! But do not expect me to accompany you. For the few days of my stay in Florence, we must part.

CHAPTER V. FROM FLORENCE TO AIX, IN SAVOY.

The beautiful road that leads from Florence to Pisa, through the vale of the Arno, that garden of Tuscany, over which, in bygone days, the diligence and the vetturino were constantly passing, might now almost be struck out of the map; for where the railroad makes its appearance the roads become next to useless, and all the poetry and all the enjoyment of travelling vanish, and only the disagreeables remain. The names of the cities and stations through which the hissing engine wings its demoniacal flight, fall only half pronounced upon the tourist's ear. A busy official is for ever opening the doors of his ambulatory prison, only to shut them again. Of the sweet village of San Donnino, the traveller, knows nothing but the name, and that only because it is written up in large letters at the station; and into the narrow streets of Signa he has no time to enter, and see the skilful industry of its strawplatting population. At Montelupo, however, he cannot help thrusting his head out at the window, for the place is so picturesque, and the river valley is so narrow and well wooded. At Empoli the train rushes on, though it is well worth stopping to see, for it is like a humming beehive, and all the inhabitants seem to live in the open air. Scarcely a glimpse is caught of the pretty town of San Miniato dei Tedeschi, the fruitful banks of the Era, or the fine shape of the mountain " Verrucca," which he has scarcely passed before the leaning tower of Pisa appears.

These sixty-nine miles took me a day and a half to travel over, but they present no great interest when compared with what I had seen before. An even and well kept road, however, is an advantage they may certainly claim. My little greyhound. " Huni," gave me so much trouble, for fear of losing her, that I determined to leave her in charge of some friends at San Giuliano, where I had been the previous year, and where she had made herself a great favourite. I had so droll an adventure with her at that time, that a relation of it may amuse my reader. This small bathing place, besides its proximity to Pisa, had the attraction of great retirement, and in the autumn of 1856, at a time when I required rest, after the completion of a work which I had had long in hand, I established myself there early in the autumn. The season was over, and of course I was much alone.

One day I was told, as something which was to give me pleasure, that in the theatre of the Casino there would be a performance that evening. " But who are the actors? " said L " Some of the townspeople," said my informant, a little offended; "and there are some very good actors among them. The admission is only two grazien, though there are some better seats at six, and you should take one of them." I was obliged to promise that I would go, and go I did; and what is more, I distributed eighty tickets amongst a crowd of persons who were at the door, but who had not the wherewithal to secure an entrance.

My little Huni followed me unperceived, and I took my seat in one of the proscenium boxes. The Italians are born actors, and one of Scribe's vaudevilles was excellently performed. Huni sat, like a judge, in a chair by my side, and observed with open mouth and perplexed eye the motions of the actors; but no sooner did she recognise in one of them the " traiteur" of the place, and in another the keeper of the casino, who were now dressed as a dancing master and his pupil, and performing the most ridiculous antics, than the little animal became unable to contain herself, and regarding neither the public, nor the orchestra, nor the footlights, she rushed to her good friends with a loud bark. Shouts of laughter and clapping of hands followed. "Vedete la Huni, la bella brava Huni!" resounded on all sides, and no prima ballerina was ever received with louder greetings.

It was now on the 13th June that I once more took leave of Pisa, one fine summer morning. My way lay northwards, across its well cultivated plains, which, however, are rather uniform and monotonous, and yet, from their garden-like character, not unpleasing to the eye. Although there was not a foot of earth uncultivated, the habitations of man were very few, and of these, many were hidden among trees. I only passed one village, " Serchio," which takes its name from the river on which it stands, which in autumn and winter frequently overflows its channel. Fifteen miles from Pisa is the town of Viareggio, where I halted for a short rest. It was here that Shelley received his classical funeral obsequies, but there is nothing, not even a wooden cross, to mark the spot. The long sandy strand, the ceaseless noise of the waves, the distant view of the fine marble mountains of Carrara, and the aromatic scent of a neighbouring pine wood, give something of a dreamy and serious character to the place. The poet will find there more to admire than the painter; and the general visitor must console himself for the want of other enjoyments with the convenience of the baths, which are close to the shore.

It was not till I, reached Pietrasanta that I took my midday refreshment. A delightful shower had laid the dust and cooled the air, and that evening ride to Carrara belongs to the fairest buds of my equestrian anthology. The road to Massa is a succession of the most luxuriant orchards and olive gardens. The white marble quarries, mixed with the hanging vines and orange trees, gave the approach to the city an appearance as uncommon as it was interesting. Not far from Massa we pass the mountain stream "Frigido," across which is a fine white marble bridge, erected by the Archduchess Maria Beatrice, the last sovereign of the little principality. The mountain "La Fose " now receives the road, and affords a splendid prospect over the valley of the Massa, the towers of the castle " Montignoso," and the rich plains beyond, stretching as far as the blue waters of the Mediterranean. After the summit is surmounted, the road then winds beneath the shade of oaks and saplings, through whose branches Carrara's amphitheatric hill, with the singular white spots which indicate the quarries, arrests the attention.

When I entered the city it was at too late an hour to think of visiting Torano and the Marble Works that evening, and I contented myself with a stroll through the town. The superfluity of white marble at every turn gives the idea of extraordinary cleanliness.

Like Ole Bull, as he entered Paris in a very splenetic humour and in the firm belief that he was to be one of the martyrs of the century, and would live nowhere but in the " Rue des Martyrs," so thought I, that under the shadow of a classic hill, which had produced the material of so many works of art, the most appropriate place of residence must be the classically named " Nuova Paros," and thither I turned my steps. My fancy did not cost me so dear as the celebrated Norwegian's did him, for he underwent the first step towards martyrdom by marrying there, yet were the accommodations of the stately and pretentious Nuova Paros so miserable, and the charges so shameless, that I cannot do better than record a warning against it.

Carrara being the last city in the duchy of Massa, we soon entered the Sardinian empire; and passing through Luna and Sarzana, we came to the banks of the Magra, that much maligned river, the passage of which is described in many a young traveller's journal in tragicomic terms of difficulty and danger. A large bridge now building will soon release them from the necessity of much fine writing! Contrary to the advice of the workmen I must needs ride over the bridge in progress: the quantity of tools and rough materials lying about was enough to make any horse shy or stumble; and I might have paid dear for my adventurous rashness, had not my horse been so sure-footed that we passed all its dangers unscathed, and Ballerina indulged in a caracole, as if pleased at his escape.

A few more miles, and the Gulf of La Spezia' in all its majesty lay before me! Gladly I greeted it, and followed its villa-decorated shores; and, fatigued with my day's journey, I sought refuge in the new hotel, " La Croce di Malta," which stands on the Parade near the water's edge. After a refreshing bath, and having laughed at the capers of the horses as Giuseppe took them into the sea, I dreamed away the evening along the pleasant margin of the beauteous gulf.

To the left, near the end of its eastern side, lay Lerici, mentioned by Dante in his " Purgatorio," and which again brought the sad fate of Shelley to my recollection, for it was to his villa there that he was returning when his boat was capsized! To the right, closing on the west side of the bay, but only visible from the sea, lies the little island of Palmaria, reminding me of Platen's charming idyll, in which he paints so well the graces of La Spezia; but then, not to deceive his friend, he adds,

" Doeh eilst du dieser Insel zu, so male dir
Nicht Capri vor, und nicht Sorrent,
Wo ewige Wollust flotet, als Sirene lanscht
Und flotet ihren Klageton."

Whether the " Freiherr von Rumohr" followed the poet's advice I never heard, but I know that, two years since, when I made the attempt to pass some time in the solitudes of that island, I found it an impossibility, seeing that there was but one house upon it, and that belonged to a Mr. Brown, who resided there with his family. This may have been the "in einer Bucht am ufer halbversteckte villa," to which Platen alludes.

During the most warlike phase of his eventful life, the great Napoleon cast his eye on the Gulf of La Spezia, as a fit place for a maritime station. It is indeed not only its beauty that gives it distinction, but its nautical and strategic safety; and in capacity it would contain the navies of all Europe. The Neapolitan Government has long contemplated the removal hither of their arsenal at Genoa. Should this ever be accomplished, the qualifications of La Spezia for a summer residence would become better known, and be soon brought into greater repute.

As it was partly the incomparable Riviera di Levante which induced me to perform my journey from Rome to Switzerland on horseback, I was now beginning to rejoice in anticipation of the splendid tract of country lying between me and Genoa, It would indeed be difficult to place its beauties before the reader. Every acre is to me a dithyrambic poem, a sublime Sabbath holiday, a hymn raised by Nature to her Maker, showing His glory in her beauties; and as poetry should be heard to be fully felt, so must the country be seen in order to awaken the admiration its magical charms deserve!

Very close behind La Spezia the road begins to assume considerable acclivity, and an occasional backward look over the Bay, which appears to be sinking lower and lower as our steps ascend, refreshes the eye, until we reach San Benedetto, or, "La Foce della Spezia." From this height the downward winding road follows the course of the river " Recco," till it flows into the Baraz. From Borghetto we traversed a hill of young chesnut trees, forming the commencement of the Pass of Beloa; and here, in the little village of Mattarana, 1,600 feet above the sea level, the Genre-painter may see one of the most tasteful female head-dresses that can be conceived, consisting of a net, in which the hair is enclosed in a very graceful manner. The geologist may also find a rich field of enjoyment here, in the quarries of

G

Italian serpentine. Ophites are found in large quantities in the chalk strata, and not far from the mountain pass this is especially the case. In the cuttings through which the road is carried, occur veins of serpentine and schillerstein, not only in the chalk, but in one another. It is remarkable that wherever serpentine exists there is always a bareness and scantiness of vegetation; and when we reach the summit of the pass, though at no more than 1,600 feet, all vegetation ceases, and the way winds between sharp spikes of rock, on which not a blade of grass is to be seen. The road itself is capitally made on both sides of the mountain, and the views, not only landward but seaward, are very fine, particularly that from the village of Bracco, where the eye wanders over the little creek of Moneglia, over Sestri, with its high promontory, over the Bay of Chiavari and the Cape of Porto Fino, and it is said that on a clear day the coast of Corsica may be distinguished.

This night I slept at Sestri di Levante, which is situated on a small isthmus at the foot of a woody promontory, and, to my mind, the most poetical spot between La Spezia and Genoa.

The country from Sestri to Rapalla so abounds in geological riches, in quiet-looking inlets, wild woodlands, and tropical looking plants, that the traveller revels in one enjoyment after another; now he strays over rocky paths, where the arbutus and the mountain-oak flourish, and from which he may glance down, hundreds of feet below, to the deep blue of the Mediterranean. Charming villas, picturesque cottages, lie strewn over the hills, while churches of characteristic architecture, with mosque-like cupolas or slender white towers, rising out of orange and lemon trees, and surrounded by aloes, fan-palms, and myrtles, show themselves from the road. Presently our way conducts us along the shore, and through fishing towns and villages, where groups of fishermen may be seen mending their nets, and women and maidens plying their lace bobbins.

It is not till we reach Nervi, with its darkcoloured houses, its fresco-covered palace, its pretty villas and blooming gardens, that this series of pictures breaks off; and after indulging a thought upon the great world-discoverer, Columbus, as we pass through Quinto, (one of the places which contend for the honour of his birth,) we shortly find ourselves at San Martino d' Albaro, which is almost a suburb of Genoa. The green spots between the houses now become smaller, and at length entirely disappear, the nearer we approach the city of palaces; and now the sun shines with unmerciful glow on the white walls, between which post-carriages, vetturini, omnibuses, and carts of all sorts stir up the thick dust in ceaseless clouds. Ah, what a weary way it is before we come to the Porta Pila!—and even when there, the endless passage over Genoa's pavement " a dos dane," which a rider on a tired horse has to endure, is enough to drive him to despair.

I alighted at the Hotel Feder, as usual; but I could not advise any one who brings his own horses to do the same, for the stables are so bad that we could not venture to use them.

Six officious waiters conducted me to the higher regions of the hotel. At every storey one of these remained behind, and the storeys seemed to have no end; and when at last I objected to go any higher, I was told, in rather a haughty tone, that His Majesty the King of Bavaria with all his suite had taken the chief part of the house. If Giuseppe had not left me I should at once have proceeded to some other hotel, but now I must submit to prosecute my ascent towards the sky, until I was left with the last of the six waiters at the landing of the sixth flight of stairs, and ushered into a small room, with nothing to console me but the balsamic thought that I was under the same roof as his Bavarian Majesty.

My garret was all but pierced through by the rays of the sun, and I began to fear that I should have to undergo the torments of a San Lorenzo. Moreover, as is usually the case in these aspiring regions, it had no means of communication with the world below. After a long wandering through all manner of passages, I found at last something like a bell on which, with the aid of my riding-whip, I rang so uninterrupted a peal, that, in a moment, a host of alarmed servants rushed up from every floor.

By means of this happy discovery I obtained an interview with Giuseppe, to whom I told my determination not to remain another day in Genoa, and that he might release my effects from the Dogana, and send them forward by diligence to Aix. The reader must not, therefore, look to me for any description of Genoa la Superba, whose beauty, as seen from the sea, ranks only after Constantinople and Naples.

The post-road between Genoa and Turin once insured the traveller an enjoyable drive. I recollect it as I have travelled over it in the paternal carriage with four horses; but, since 1854, when the railway was opened, this road, like those I have before alluded to, is blotted out of the traveller's note book. Here again what beauties does he not miss, and what interest does he not lose, in his flight through tunnels and cuttings!

But though I was seated on my Ballerino, in glorious freedom, and in the enjoyment of all that nature could afford me, it took three days to accomplish a distance which the locomotive dashes over in six hours; and although I thought of the interest comprised in those three days, and that I had visited Alessandria's citadel, and Alfieri's birthplace, I felt the difference between riding 120 Italian miles on the back of a spirited horse, and lounging over them on the soft cushions of a railroad carriage, and I will not deny that I welcomed the approach to Turin with much satisfaction, and, with still more the hospitalities of the Hotel de la Grande Bretagne!

As I entered the hotel, an " affiche monstre " caught my attention, announcing the last performance of Ciniselli for that evening, and I had heard so much of this famous rider, that I could not resist the temptation of seeing him. Ciniselli was for a long time one of Franconi's troop, but he can now boast of a company of his own, fully equal to that of his master. The perfection to which he has brought the art, as shewn in the management and instruction of his horse " Monte Cristo," has lately added to his renown. This " Monte Cristo " is a fine English horse, which the King of Sardinia had purchased for £400, for his own use; but, as the skill of all his roughriders had failed in overcoming the vice and untameable wildness of the animal (I am of course speaking of anteRarey times), he was sold for a very insignificant sum to Ciniselli, who has succeeded in obtaining the mastery over him to such a degree as to render him perfectly docile and intelligent. On the present occasion Monte Cristo was not to perform, but I paid him a visit in his stable, where he stood so quietly that it seemed scarcely credible that four men were at one time required to perform his daily toilette.

Besides Signora Ciniselli, there was a little girl from Hungary, who was called " Bertha," and who had been sold by her parents to Ciniselli, and seemed likely to do the greatest credit to his instructions. With a grace, skill, and precision which the goddesses of the circus do not always possess, she performed that evening greater " Hauttaits " than I ever saw at Franconi's! But what most interested me was Ciniselli himself, in plain clothes, on a proud mare, exhibiting the art of equitation; and it was wonderful to see how, without spur, or even a switch, but only with a slight pressure of his leg, he put the elegant " Vittoria" through all her paces!

Two days later, and I was mounting Ballerino, at Susa, on a fine morning, just as the sun was overcoming the cool freshness of the night air, and commencing my ascent of Mount Cenis. This pass of the Alps, though most in use, is certainly the longest and the least interesting of any. But if it offer to the epicurean tourist no " Via Mala," no " Devil's Bridge," no " Priest's Leap," and such like fantastic scenes, the true lover of true nature will still find in it a rich repast, as, step by step, he follows a road abounding in curves and windings, and defiles of every kind, until, from a height of 7000 feet, his astounded gaze seems to light upon a new zone.

And is not the road itself an object of admiration and wonderment, as a monument of the imperial engineer, Napoleon? At his command it was begun in 1803, and finished in 1810, at an expenditure of seven millions and a half of francs.

An inn, called the " Grande Croix," and a group of buildings for the use of guides and muleteers, showed me that I was at the highest point of the pass. The perpetual wind that blows on every mountain top greeted us with true alpine severity as we rode along the little plain at the extremity of which stands the Hospice, founded in the ninth century by Charles the Great, who crossed the mountain with his whole army. The present building is the work of Napoleon. One-half of it is inhabited by a corps of carabineers, whose duty is to examine passports; and the other half by a few Benedictine monks, who dispense their gratuitous hospitality to the poorer class of travellers.

I proceeded onwards to the more distant posthouse, close to a little lake, which is completely frozen for six months in the year, and where most delicious trout are caught. A sundial with the Latin inscription "Tempus irreparabile fugit" surprised me not a little, and I was entering the house to inquire who was the originator of it, when such an icy-cold blast came from the room, that I rushed back into the open air to have the benefit of the sunshine. Walking along the margin of the lake, I saw crocuses, forget-me-nots, and gentianella in full bloom! But, alas, it was no longer under an Italian sky that I was walking! The sun sank down, and the grey clouds gathered over head, and a freezing wind rippled the leadcoloured surface of the water, and I felt such a feverish sickness at the sudden change, that I was obliged to seek refuge in a room of the inn, where before a bright fire, and wrapped up with every thing I had with me, I sought to recover myself with warm wine and water, sufficiently to be able to abandon this unfriendly region as soon as the horses were ready to proceed.

I hoped we might soon reach a more genial clime, and little thought what an exhausting journey was before me! We had not long left the inn when the heavy clouds began to unload themselves of a mixture of snow, hail, and rain. At the same time an icy wind blew so strongly, that it was next to impossible to sit my horse. I therefore dismounted, took the little puppy under my shawl, gave my horse to Giuseppe, and looping up the skirt of my habit, I prepared to walk the eight miles to Lanslebourg. I could not have supposed that, at the end of June, so stormy a walk could be possible. To shorten the way, I took a side path, and now I found myself in a thicket of thorn bushes, out of which I could hardly make my escape; and then among the long meadow-grass, which wetted me nearly to the waist; now over a rough, rocky path, where a false step might have precipitated me into a chasm; and then wading through a mountain brook, all the while beaten by rain and hail so unmercifully that I could scarcely keep my eyes open. My little dog, however, warm and untroubled by what was going on around him, slept at his ease, not dreaming that he was passing over a road where, years ago, one of his kind was snapped up and devoured by a wolf, before the very eyes of his master—Horace Walpole.

I was in a terrible condition when I arrived at Lanslebourg, and I felt the more painfully the deficiencies of the hotel there—added to which the house was under repair, and the landlady a sour, unobliging person. The only habitable room could not be entered without danger to life and limb in the transit, owing to the number of things I had to stride over! My clothes were so wet that the night was not long enough to dry them; and as we had now nothing to fear from heat, I did not start so early in the morning as usual.

I found nothing particular to remark till I arrived at the Castle of Lesseillon, which, with its ranges of batteries one above another, commands this pass into Italy, and takes the part which the fortress of La Brunetta at Susa formerly played. A light bridge stretched across the ravine cannot fail of attracting attention here, being one which might very appropriately be called " The Devil's."

At Modane, the last scene in Sterne's " Sentimental Journey," we took our midday rest, and afterwards crossed the valley of Maurienne. The near and distant, small and large, bald and wooded hills which surround it, present much variety to the traveller, but to its poor inhabitants they offer no reward for their industry, but a scanty vintage, which is obtained only by great care and much toil.

We had to ride a long distance to-day, and it was late at night when we arrived at St. Jean, where, however, the friendly reception we met with, and the cleanliness and order of everything in the "Hotel de l'Europe," quickly banished all idea of fatigue from my mind.

We were now but fifty miles from Aix les Bains, and two days' ride would enable us to accomplish this distance with ease. My first night quarters were at Montmeillan, in the neighbourhood of which town a delicious white wine is made. Montmeillan stands at the junction of four roads: one from Mount Cenis over the vale of Maurienne—one from the Little St. Bernard—one from Grenoble—and one from Chambery. Its castle long served Savoy as a bulwark against France, but a few rugged stones, overgrown with nettles and thorns, are all that now remains of the fortress.

Chambery was my next point, and willingly did I rest my eye on the beautiful prospect from the terraces of the Castle of Berneez, and on the Elephant Fountain, a memorial which the townspeople have raised to their philanthropic fellow citizen, General de Boigne. St. Real, and the novelist Favier de Maistre, were also born here, and a part of my stay was devoted to " Les Charmettes," the dwelling of Jean Jacques Rousseau, and his friend Madame Warens. Fancy, however, must have created much of my pleasure, for the cottage and its miserable rooms were little worthy of such an owner.

My evening ride to Aix was extremely pleasant, looking over the Lake of Bourget, and the mountain chain of the " Mont du Chat."

All that the height of the season could give to Aix les Bains, aristocratic " elegants" and " elegantes," pleasure-seeking cits, and the ordinary class of bathing-place frequenters, enlivened the scene, on the fine summer evening when I rode up the principal street to the "place centrale." Here everybody seemed jumbled together, some in carriages, some on foot, some on asses, and some sitting in chairs, but none on horseback; while troops of smoking, drinking, gambling, and staring " lions" surrounded the cafes, all gazing with curious eyes upon the dusty equestrian arrival.

Having the address of several "pensions," I determined to try them first; but our appearance not being at all enticing, " the house is quite full" was the only reply I received, so that I gave up the attempt and rode off to the Casino Street, and the " Hotel Guilland."

The sight of my trunks, which now arrived from the Diligence Bureau, acted like magic, and the at first mistrustful looks of the landlady were changed to smiles and welcomes. The folding doors of two pretty rooms flew open, and tea was served with Parisian elegance and celerity; but, I had to pay well for it!

CHAPTER VI. AIX LES BAINS, IN SAVOY.

" Quand vous arriverez aux Eaux minerales, faites comme si vous entriez dans le Temple d'Eseulape; laissez a la porte toutes les passions qui occupent votre esprit."— *Dr. Alibert.*

Should ever design or chance lead you to Aix, and should you walk on the Chambery road, please to notice a group of poor-looking houses over against the elegant " Hotel du Prince," and you will see on one of them the following inscription—

" Davat, Aubergiste, loge a pied." having the representation of two billiard queues underneath it; and on the next house—

" Pension Veuve Perroux."

In this " bicoque," the reader, if it concern him to know more of my fate, may now seek me. Let him not hesitate to mount the steep ladder-like steps which lead from the street into this one-storied dwelling, and a very few more will bring him into an airy gallery, whence he will overlook the very room in which I am now sitting. I would also ask him to give a glance over the neighbouring porte cochere of the house of Madame Perroux. In a cool, lofty, and freshstrewn stable, he will observe my faithful servants Ballerino and Baffoni, enjoying their rest and their oats at the same time. There also may be observed my little greyhound puppy, running about from one corner to another, till the deep voice of the Corese, and his "Alio cuccio, al posto tuo," sends him at once to his post between the two horses, where he amuses himself by snapping at their noses. The proud satisfaction with which the Corese overlooks his little kingdom, where he keeps so much order and propriety, is also worth looking at; and, if he had not made friends with some Piedmontese soldiers whom he has invited to cards this evening, he would perhaps initiate you into the mysteries of his stable economy.

But these happy results were not attained without trouble and pains. The difficulties in the way of obtaining a good stable, and the shameless demands of the hotel and pension keepers, would have soon sent me away from Aix. After two days' troublesome and fruitless search, I was walking in the cool of the evening on the road to Chambery, turning over in my mind what other baths there were in Savoy or Switzerland assimilating to those of Aix, when one of those sharp-eyed personages who are always prowling about in search of new arrivals proposed to me the " Widow Perroux" and her "pension. " The man's respectable appearance induced me to try his recommendation.

On our arrival at the house, he first conducted me into a kitchen, where everything looked clean, and was in its proper place. The worthy widow herself superintended all the stewing, the boiling, the baking, and the roasting, with every appearance of knowing what she was about. There was an aroma in the room which seemed to show an artist's hand in what she was then mixing, that would probably have satisfied a Liebig.

As I entered, the widow Perroux was inspecting the doings of her adjutante, (who, being an undoubted Savoyarde, must of course be named Jeanette,) and she conducted me into another chamber which was devoted to the preparation of her master-pieces. She then took me up the ladder-like stairs to the storey above, and opened before me a large book, in which a host of French nobility had certified to her culinary skill and her attention to her guests, and then she began to bring her persuasive powers to bear upon me, to induce me to take up my abode in her house. She did not find it a difficult task, for everything was exceedingly tempting, and the little room which opened out of the gallery, the neighbourhood of the Casino gardens, and the capital stable already described, all seemed so alluring, that the following morning I removed myself and all my possessions to the modest locality where the reader has already discovered me.

My next care was to seek out Dr. Despine, in order to have his directions about the course of bathing which I was to undertake. His family name has been well known for three generations to all the faculty in France and Piedmont, but especially at Aix. The present possessor of the name and reputation, Dr. Baron Despine, I found to be a most interesting person, well acquainted with art, literature, and archaeology; and his enthusiasm for Italy soon placed us on a friendly footing together. Having given me his professional advice, he offered, in the most cordial manner, his services as cicerone, whenever I shall feel inclined to visit the Roman remains; and the excursion which a few days later I made in his company is among my most pleasant recollections of Aix les Bains.

Germany is so rich in the possession of baths and healing springs, and eminent physicians also, that the mineral waters of other lands are thrown somewhat in the shade by them. But Aix will ever be of importance, even to German invalids, from the superiority of its climate over that of any of the northern bathing-places. The pass of Mont Cenis, already begun, and the proposed junction of the French, Italian, and Helvetic railways, promise these springs a brilliant future; and for this reason what I shall have to say about Aix will be much to the purpose.

Aix—Aqua? Allobrogum, Gratianse, or Domitianse of the ancients—lies in one of the fairest valleys of Savoy, and is enclosed by two mountain chains on the north and on the southern side. Their rugged peaks, some of which are 5000 feet high, contrast most favourably with the gracefully rounded hill under whose shelter the town is built. The number of its inhabitants is something above 4000, but during the season it is more than doubled.

In the time of the Romans, Aix was incorporated with Allobrogum. After it came into the possession of Rudolf III. , King of Burgundy, it was an object of contest between the Duchess of Savoy and the Count of Genf, but a treaty concluded in 1295 left it the property of the former, who raised it to a barony, and afterwards to a marquisate.

In its castle, which was founded in the sixteenth century, there are three epochs, or changes of destiny, distinctly traceable. A temple of Diana formed the foundation of its great tower, and thus far it is ancient. Its remarkable and well preserved staircase is of the Gothic-Arabic period, and it is modern as regards its Italian ball-room. The tower contains a theatre. The building is now the property of the Marquis d'Aix Commariva, and it served as a casino from 1824 to 1849. The bath buildings which Victor Amadee III. erected in 1773, and the new casino, with its beautiful gardens, erected by a joint-stock company, are next in magnitude to the castle. It is quite superfluous to say much of the mineral springs, as such descriptions are not very interesting to the general reader, and all medical men can obtain whatever information they require from Dr. Despine's " Indicateur Medicale et Topographique." I shall, therefore, confine myself to the cursory statement that, besides the two sulphur and alum springs, Aix has several others in its neighbourhood. It is worthy of remark, that nature has given to these two chief springs a temperature exactly suited to the animal economy. At Leuk, Carlsbad, Aqui, Lamothe, and other places, the water wells out of the earth at so high a degree of heat that it cannot be used without cooling. At Harrogate, Schinznach, Uriage, and Allevard, on the other hand, the temperature is too low, and it must be artificially raised. In both cases some of the gas escapes, and a part of the healing virtue is lost. Again, in many places the water has to be drawn by machinery, and the least disorder in that machinery suddenly cuts off the supply. The springs of Aix bubble out half way up the hill, and can be made to shoot up from 1 to 30 feet. The mean temperature is 35 Reaumur, and the supply is very great.

The climate of Aix is mild.and pure. The Flora of the neighbourhood is quite that of a southerly clime; and that the fig, the almond, the peach, the mulberry, and the pomegranate grow so luxuriantly, may in some measure be attributed to the form of the hill, and the warm springs by which it is watered.

Although Aix is resorted to by a vast number of pleasure seekers and invalids with much advantage, and the rich tourist may have every comfort and convenience there, I can never think of my stay in the place with any satisfaction. One can submit to the tyrannic demands of a course of bathing when one has the assurance of a happy result; but this failed me entirely: and that worn out sophistical assertion, that in proportion to the discomfort you suffer from the process of the cure will be the benefit afterwards derived from it, was no consolation to me. I found myself so weakened from the effects of the bath, that the lightest employment was a task. The heat, which was very great that year, doubtless added to my debility. The thermometer, which hung on the shady gallery, was seldom under, and often above, 29 Reaumur, at midday; and the wooden bicoque of the widow Perroux was so heated by the sun, that 1 often had recourse to the cool stable for a change.

Between Aix at six in the morning, and Aix at six in the evening, there was as vast a difference as between the morning negligee and the evening toilette of a " sur le retour" bordering beauty. In the evening you see the same fashionables in all the plenitude of modern dress, stiff silks, transparent gauzes, and coquettish hats, thronging the gardens and the roads, on foot or in carriages, whom, in the rosy morning, you had encountered with pale and sunken features, being drawn from their dwellings to the bath-house in " chaises a porteurs. "

To avoid such sights, I made my arrangements to take my baths at home, and, therefore, I will not trouble my readers with the relation of the curious processes that these poor people went through in the temple of Hygeia, but rather proceed to call his attention to the fine environs of Aix.

Besides the shady gardens of the new and old casino, and several private grounds which visitors have leave to use, there are many other walks and drives, some near and others more distant. Among the former I must mention the Port du Puer, a small haven, approached by an avenue of Italian poplars, 1,500 metres long, and whence the little steam boats start which navigate the lake of Bourget. Then, there is "La Tour de M. Eustache," close to the ferruginous well of St. Simon. " La Maison du Diable," a lofty and solitary building, from which you obtain a splendid view, the name being derived (says the legend) from a spiritual tenant, who enticed thither an innocent shepherdess, and kept her concealed there. " La Colline de Tresserve," with the fine property of the late Oberstein Biviand, which has a double prospect, over the valley of Aix on one side, and the lake of Bourget on the other. The vine-covered " Cote de St. Innocent," and the " Cascade de Gresy," at the confluence of the Sierroz and the Dissi, with its dreadful tale of the early death of Baroness von Brock, in the sight of her friend Queen Hortense! The visit to the " Mont du Chat" is rather a more distant, but one of the most interesting excursions of the place. According to Polybius it was here that Hannibal, in the year 220 before Christ, crossed the mountains, when, on his march to Rome, he made his way through the country of the Allobroges. Many Roman coins have been picked up here,

H and if I do not mistake, an inscription dedicated to Mercury.

The ascent of the Dent du Chat amply repays the trouble. It is a rocky cone of 1600 metres high, from the top of which one of the most distant, as well as beautiful, views is to be had. But unequal at this time to all these fatigues, I was obliged to content myself with a gentle voyage on the lake. Do not expect, however, that the little steamer which undertakes this trip will compare with the fine boats of the Rhine or the Swiss lakes. No deck awning protects you from the sun, no fine band of music, no display of delicate refreshments enhances the pleasures of the day; and truly you will not run the risk of the eccentric Englishman of overlooking the scenery, owing to the charms of the " cotelettes." Here you may rejoice when there is *no* band, and if you are not obliged by absolute thirst to have recourse to bad beer!

In the beauty of the lake, however, which may be taken in at one glance from end to end, of the wooded hills and the ancient castles that surround it, you may find much to admire, even if you have visited the Rhine and Switzerland. Look, now, how the Castles of Bonport, Bordeau, and Chatelle stand out! How, with every turn of the paddlewheel, the contour of the old abbey of Haute Combe varies! This abbey has given three saints to the Calendar, two popes to the Chair of St. Peter, and many a celebrated cardinal and prelate. Its architecture presents no very marked feature of beauty; but the octangular tower which rises at its side, its perfect solitude and contemplative stillness, combine to form an incomparable picture. After a two hours' voyage the steamboat runs into an inlet, and discharges its passengers into the shady walks and cool cloisters of the abbey. It was founded by Amadee III., in 1125, as a place of sepulture for the House of Savoy, and many high personages rest there. It was first inhabited by monks of the order of St. Basil, but its retired situation did not shield it from the consequences of the Revolution; and in 1793 it was laid waste. Not till 1824 was it restored by the devout King Charles Felix, and in 1843 it was given to the Cistercian friars. The church has been well restored by good artists; among its monuments are the tombs of King Charles Felix and his queen Maria Christina.

You must not leave Haute Combe without seeing the "Fontaine Intermittente." A path shaded by chestnuts and planes conducts one over a gentle rise to the spot; and when you have paid homage to the nymph of the fountain, the turf of her domain forms a capital place for a picnic!

If the Flora of the valley of Aix delights the botanist, and the exploration of its hills and caves the geologist, no less do the " twenty-three different sorts of fish" which abound in the lake charm the gastronomist. It is enough to mention the " salmo umbra," the " salmo alpinus," the " gadus lota," and the " perca fluviatiiis."

It was under peculiarly favourable circumstances that I now inspected these scenes, for I was accompanied by Dr. Despine, whose knowledge of everything relating to them is very extensive. The Roman Baths, the Campanus Arch, and the Temple of Diana are the chief antiquities at Aix. Among the first, the most remarkable sight is the " Vaporarium," discovered beneath the " Pension Chabert." It is octangular in form, and round its interior are white marble " scallaria," or steps. One hundred pillars support a gallery, and in the ceiling above are numerous small outlets, through which the vapour ascended to an upper vaporarium, or a bath.

A large basin, in which Henry IV. and all his followers bathed in the year 1600, has retained the name of " Bain Royal " to this day. In the centre there is a remnant of a pedestal, on which no doubt a statue formerly stood.

On the way to this bath stands the Campanus Arch. It is in good preservation, and still forms an ornament to the city. Inscriptions on the architrave and plinth inform us that it was erected in honour of the " Familia Pompeia."

At a short distance from the baths, according to the Roman custom, stands a temple, the socalled " Temple of Diana. " It is much sunken in the ground, but is accessible on two sides.

A tolerable collection of mosaics, amphorae, fragments of statues, bas-reliefs, and columns of porphyry and serpentine, may be seen at the house of M. Chabert.

A sight of a different kind, and scarcely less worthy of inspection, is the Pathological Collection of Dr. Despine, consisting of wax modellings of parts of the human frame in health and disease.

Since I left Aix, I have heard with much gratification that the "Administration Superieure des Bains " has, in consideration of the services of the three generations of the Despine family to their native town, decided on giving their name to a part of the contemplated Institution for Bathing. This promising building was intended to be ready for the season of 1859.

CHAPTER VII.

Departure From Aix.—Grotto De Bange.— Annech On The 9th, And Lucerne On The 29th August, 1857.

Whatever advantages Aix may offer as a bathing place, or as a summer residence, I cannot deny that I felt a pleasurable sensation when, after a six weeks' sojourn there, I greeted the day of my departure.

The earliest of the early risers were yet asleep, and all was still and silent in the town, when, between four and five on a splendid August morning, I rode out of the Place Centrale. The green blinds of the neat houses were all closed, and the twitter of an harmonious bird chorus, coming from the dark trees of the " Promenade des Maronniers," was the only sound that fell upon my ear.

" A ne plus nous revoir," I was almost on the point of exclaiming to the venerable chesnuts, in imitation of some French soldiers on leaving Rome, who, with true French light-heartedness, so addressed the Roman women who were lamenting their departure.

But I must now beg my reader to accompany me in a little digression which I am about to make to a very remarkable, but scarcely known place. While I was in Aix, a Savoyard, from the vale of Cheran, gave me a somewhat fantastic description of the "Grotto de Bange," which determined me not to leave unseen this little-visited natural curiosity, notwithstanding some sacrifice of time in going so much out of my way.

Soon after passing the fountain of St. Simon we left the high road and struck into a shady path on the right hand of it. The valley through which it led us became narrow and more narrow, until we reached the village of Cusy. Here we turned into the valley of Cheran, where our prospect began to extend itself. The high hills of Cusy on the right, and those of Alleve on the left, suddenly seemed to recede, and allowed the eye to delight itself with their well-covered slopes. But we were now quite deprived of shade. The insects made martyrs of our horses, and when about an hour's ride from Cusy, we discovered, with dismay, that the path divided into two!

Without any map of the country, and without a hope of meeting a creature of whom to make an inquiry; suffering from the heat of the sun, and dispirited by the houseless valley, I began to reproach myself with imprudence in having undertaken this trip without a guide. I selected, quite by chance, the left-hand branch, and it was fortunate I did so, for in about a quarter of an hour we met a man who was going to Cusy! " Is this the way to the Grotto de Bange?" shouted I, before we came up to him. "Why," said he, "are you going there?"

" What should prevent me? "

" Oh! nothing. But only it is lucky we met, since I alone have the keys to the grotto, and you could not have seen it in my absence! On Sundays and holidays I always carry my fish to one of the neighbouring villages, and I was now on my way to Cusy; but I will give up my intention, and conduct you to the grotto."

This rencontre with the Savoyard, who de

H 3 scribed himself as a fisherman and custodier of the Grotto de Bange, had a double value to me: first, in providing me with the means of reaching the spot without further mistakes; and secondly, in the prospect of some of his trout for my midday meal!

I endeavoured to bring down Ballerino's elastic step to the heavy tread of the fisherman, and " strado facendo," I got him to tell me much about the grotto and the subterranean waters. To my astonishment I learned that last season only two strangers, and this year not one, had visited it! Neither had curiosity ever induced this plain peasant to visit Aix; and it was a matter of surprise to find such naivete, and, at the same time, so much knowledge of the world, as the fisherman Pierre possessed.

" But who lent you this fine horse? " said he, after a pause.

" It is my own," said I.

" Yours!" he replied. " But who are you? Your figure, your features, and your speech are those of a lady; but a lady can hardly possess two such handsome animals as these! And why do you sit as if you only had one leg? Why does all this long cloth hang down on one side? and is that gentleman who follows you dumb, that he does not say a word?"

It would have been as vain to have tried to give this son of nature any idea of cultivated life, as it would be to afford my readers any notion of his unsophisticated conversation. He amused me greatly, and I was almost sorry when we reached his dwelling, which he had built with his own hands, in a field between two hills, and which consisted of but two rooms— one for himself and his family, and one for his cow.

I had scarcely entered when the busy Pierre uttered a kind of " jodeln " cry, which he told me was a signal to his son, who was gone to the neighbouring village, that a stranger had arrived, and that he must bring two of his companions, it being forbidden that he should show the cave to any body unless three men were with them.

After we had left the field, we entered a young wood, the moist atmosphere of which, and the fine carpet of turf covered with cyclamen, forget-me-nots, and strawberry blossoms, were so enjoyable, that more than once I sat down on the root of a tree, and we were three-quarters of an hour in reaching the grotto.

With an important air, Maitre Pierre opened the door of his subterranean kingdom, and the other men having lighted some torches, we all entered. The passage at first was so small that we could only walk in single file; and the slipperiness of the floor made walking very difficult, particularly as it was impossible to keep one's eyes from the millions of sparkling objects above our heads. Pierre told me that the caverns and the wood belonged to a peasant named Moine, and that he had sold it to a speculator who thought to make his fortune by the sale of the gold which the sands contained; but who had been wofully deceived, for that out of four kilos of sand, no more than twenty centimes worth of gold could be extracted!

After walking twelve or fifteen minutes the cave became larger, and we were now standing in a good-sized room. "Here," said Pierre, "in the time of religious persecutions, sixty years ago, mass was performed. But it was not always put to so good a use, for about thirty years back a gang of coiners executed their unlawful work in it, until discovered and sent to the galleys."

" I should think the life of the galleys preferable to that which they were leading here."

"Ah, dear lady, the Grotto de Bange has seen worse scenes than that! Only fourteen days ago, as, in the absence of other occupation, I was washing for gold on the sea-shore, the corpse of a young girl came out with the stream, and that is not the *only* one I have seen! Neither the place of the outflow nor the extent of the subterranean lake are known. Some think it goes as far as Annech, and that it is connected with that lake; but it is equally possible that it may extend much farther. Just listen! and you will hear what an unearthly noise the rush of the water, and the current of winds, make! Might we not suppose it the groans and cries of all who have found their death here?"

" Truly," said I, " in the world below there can hardly be anything more fearful; but somebody told me there was a boat here!"

" A boat there is," said Pierre, " but I would not advise its use."

The shrieks of the spirits became louder as we proceeded, until at last our guide cried " Halt!" and peremptorily forbade our going farther. "The water,"said he, "is higher than usual, and is already up to my feet, and the boat has broken adrift, and been carried away with the stream."

We lowered our torches and saw that it was as he said, and then I told him that we had better make our way back; for I was fully satisfied with this Dante-like episode! And oh! how refreshing it was once more to see the light of day, and breathe the free air of heaven, and enjoy the warmth of the sun again!

We had only just entered the hut when Pierre began to put on his Sunday clothes, in rder, as he told me, to go to the village and procure me some bread and wine. Meantime;he son prepared the fish; and I may say that eldom has a meal tasted so gratefully to my lalate as did the fine trout and the brown oread under the humble roof of Maitre Pierre, and it was not the least part of the pleasure to see him and his family enjoy so much better food than they were used to. The two bottles of wine so exhilarated the party, that they would hardly allow us to depart. "At least," said Pierre, " I must accompany you to Alleve, for it is a way which may easily be mistaken."

My conductor told me that the river which waters this valley and flows into the Rhone carries with it a quantity of gold dust, which is carefully sought for by the people of several places through which it passes.

We rode along by the side of the mountain chain of Cusy, and Alleve soon became visible, with its picturesque church and fantastically formed " Tour de St. Jaques," which name is given to a curious mass of rock, rising sharply and boldly in the midst of the plain, reminding me vividly of the "Faraglioni" in Capri. Maitre Pierre said that the ascent to its top was so difficult that it had not been undertaken for many years, except by the men who are periodically employed to cut the wood that grows upon it, and then it is done by the help of ladders.

At Alleve I bade the worthy fisherman a hearty farewell, and gave him a liberal reward for all his trouble, as well as an assurance that I would recommend him and his cavern to all my acquaintance who might come this way.

The views now extended themselves, and became more interesting every mile we rode over; and when we had mounted a certain height on the " Gruffy," we came to a panorama which after-experience showed me was not surpassed in Savoy.

Passing through many wretched villages, whose condition contrasted sadly with the richness of the country in which they stand, we came at length to the high road from Chambery to Annech; a name which awakens recollections of the great author of the " Confessions," and with animation and enthusiasm I greeted the point from which a first glimpse of his house can be obtained.

The dark clouds of grief hung over the usually cheerful-looking town of Annech on that 9th of August. " What common cause of trouble can it be that is so visible in the faces of all these thoughtful-looking people? Has Savoy lost one of her chief sons?" So thought I to myself as I rode through the streets to the Hotel de Geneve.

" No," was the reply to my inquiry; " the man we mourn was a foreigner, but a foreigner who possessed greatness of soul and nobleness of heart in the highest degree in which they ever distinguished manhood, or served the cause of freedom."

It was Eugene Sue, the great French novelist, who had expired but a few hours before.

There was his freshly-closed grave, covered with flowers and garlands, and there the people around it still, uttering words of condolence with each other. Whether the feverish productions of his glowing fancy have tended to the happiness and good of his fellow-men, who shall decide? The depth and richness of that fancy are matter of universal wonder and admiration. A mourning people are now around me. I hear the sighs and I see the tears of Savoy, and such tears can only be shed for a noble and excellent man. Struck with the moving scene, I felt my own eyes dimmed with emotion. Rest, then, in peace, with thy great heart and thy great spirit! Rest softly in that Savoy land which thou hast known and loved, and which has known and loved thee, and which will guard thy remains with pride until the day, perchance, arrive when thy own fatherland shall claim them! Those bright hopes in which thou didst place thy strong faith will then be fulfilled.

Eugene Sue came to Savoy in order that, in the solitude of its beautiful mountains, he might find that rest which his native land denied him. He resided near to Annech, in a country-house, his own property, called " Les Barattes." Resigned to his fate, he lived the last six years of his existence secluded from the world, and, devoting daily nine hours to his labours, he spent the remainder of the day in doing good. The world still received his literary productions with eager delight; but those who approached him in his adopted country loved him chiefly for his good heart and patient resignation, and he had a kind and a helping hand for misfortune of every sort. The decree for his banishment was his death-blow. It is difficult to pluck out the love of country from a manly breast. It surpasses, in some at least, all other love. It raises the man into the great and virtuous patriot, and is far from growing cold in exile. Eugene Sue had a morbid disposition and a too sensitive soul. He could not bear up against a sorrow so bitter; and the mere thought of his country plunged him into the deepest melancholy. He lived in a foreign land, free, beloved, and protected, but it was not his native land.

After an illness of three days, he expired in his fifty-third year. He died, as he had lived, a freethinker, and was buried in that portion of the cemetery appropriated to the heterodox. Such a funeral train as followed his body Savoy had never seen. It was like an apotheosis. From the rising ground where his dwelling stood, to the very gate of the churchyard, there was an uninterrupted crowd of weeping people. Mons.Caillard, his brother-in-law, and the Oberst Charras, one of the worthiest heads of the Democratic party, on whose breast Eugene Sue had breathed his last sigh, headed the procession which conducted the great writer, the honourable man, and the enlightened patriot, to his last home.

The following day I arrived at Geneva. First the " Pont de Caille," a fine hanging bridge of iron over the Ussus; then the interesting environs of Mont Saleve; then the prospect over the rich and well-cultivated Arvethal; and at last the distant view of the classic Leman. These were the several gradations of this charming ride. Everything breathes prosperity, industry, and cultivation, as soon as we have stepped over the boundary of Savoy.

Of course it is not my purpose to say much of the well-known and beautiful Helvetia. In this Garden of Europe one can meet with no adventure. Here there is nothing but security and comfort, excellent roads, and a superfluity of incomparable hotels.

The sublime book of Alpine nature has inspired too many to need being quoted again by me. I must therefore fling my pen into the Lethe waters of the fair Leman, and, armed only with my riding wand, prosecute my journey in speculative contemplation through the smiling land.

When I reached Langnau I thought I would give the horses a good rest; and therefore I told Giuseppe that I should remain there till the day after the morrow; but he assured me we could easily go on the next day, as Baffoni was so well he could hardly hold him in as he took him to the farrier's. The greater, therefore, was my surprise when I was told, the very same evening, that the poor thing would not eat, and that symptoms of serious illness had appeared.

The next morning Giuseppe tapped at my door, with the doubly disagreeable intelligence that the horse was no better, and that a heavy rain was falling.

" What, then, are we to do? "

" My advice, Signora, is that we should clothe Baffoni well, and start as soon as the rain diminishes. In six hours we shall be at Lucerne, where a good stable and proper advice will soon recover him."

There was literally nothing else to be done; and as no other horse could be hired, Giuseppe must walk. We accordingly put this plan into execution, and two hours later we all stood before the " Golden Lamb," an isolated wayside inn.

" How far is it to Lucerne?" asked I of the landlord.

" To Lucerne!" replied he, " why you have come all the way from Wohlhusen out of your way! It is but two hours' journey from that place to Lucerne, but it is four from this! This is Menznau!"

I cannot say how this news disturbed me. I, who would have given any money to have shortened the poor animal's walk, by this unlucky mistake had thus so greatly lengthened it!

" Alas! for the poor horse," said the host, " he is indeed very ill, and you should get him to Lucerne as soon as you can."

Again we set forward on our sad march. We wrapped him in everything we had to lay over him; and mounted on my own horse, I led Baffoni by the bridle, while Giuseppe followed in a " char de cote," lent me by the landlord: and thus, after a weary and anxious time, we reached our goal, and little did I care for the comments of the Lucerners as we passed through the town!

For three days after my arrival at Bellerive the poor horse occupied our hopes and fears. Those only who share my love of animals, and who know the gratitude we owe to such faithful servants, will participate in my anxiety.

In the elegant rooms of the Villa Bellerive all was silent; the lamps, all but one, had been extinguished, and in the gloomy light that *one* afforded, the figures in the pictures on the walls seemed to come out of their frames. The last stroke of midnight had sounded from the beautiful rococo timepiece, and all was still again. But hark! a distant bay of dogs; a wellknown neigh! Oh, Ballerino, why that anxious cry?

I hurried to the window; a majestic peacefulness was spread over the sleeping face of nature. The moonbeams played upon the smooth waters of the lake; and Mount Pilatus, in dark sublimity, seemed to be dreaming of the ancient greatness of the Helvetic race.

A light appeared through the young chesnut alley. What means that group of men, that midnight train?

It was Baffoni's funeral! A grave, granted by an affectionate brother to a sister's favourite, in a retired corner of his fair domain, received the remains of her faithful servant!

Reader, what more is left for me to tell? That 29th of August was the last of the " 101 days " I had proposed to describe to you; and in the same grave where rest Baffoni's bones, lies buried many a bright hope whose blossoms were destined for your amusement. All idea of my Spanish tour is at an end!

I must therefore console myself with " A Visit to the Island of La Maddalena. " GARIBALDI AT HOME.

A VISIT TO THE MEDITERRANEAN ISLANDS OF LA MADDALENA AND CAPRERA.

INTRODUCTION.

Among the artists who graced Rome with their presence during the winter of 1849— that winter so prolific of political hopes and vicissitudes—there came one, whose extraordinary performance on the mandolin excited the greatest astonishment and delight. His name was Vimercati, an affable old man, whose courteous manners drew forth as much friendly sympathy as his beautiful music inspired admiration.

Myself initiated in the difficulties of the mandolin, I was, perhaps more than others of his audiences, enraptured with the marvellous tones which he brought out of his instrument. I sought his acquaintance, and he soon became one of my most assiduous visitors.

One evening, as I was surrounded by a little circle of friends, my virtuoso so completely surpassed himself, that I could not help asking him what could possibly have induced him to devote his incomparable talent to so ungrateful an instrument?

His reply was charmingly naive. " Madam," said he, "it was precisely because all other artists seemed to despise the poor mandolin that I declared myself its champion, and determined to rescue it from what has so long been its fate, the accompaniment of the vulgar songs of the common people."

My dear reader, I hope, will not think that I have the presumption to compare the feeble powers of my pen with the musical genius of the master of whom I have spoken; but, in calling public attention to the insignificant island of Maddalena, a rock that has been almost forgotten since the time of the Romans, I fancy I hear a murmur of surprise, to which, adopting the idea of my friend Vimercati, I would answer " It, is precisely because *it is* so neglected and forgotten, and that it is the only one of the Mediterranean Isles that has not found an explorer and describer, that I have determined to make its beauties and attractions my theme."

Corsica, enveloped in the magic veil of its historical past, has become well known to us by the recent work of Gregorovius. Sardinia can boast the classic pages of La Marmora. Elba has been described by M. Valery. Sicily by Parthei, Mrs. Power, and others. Capraja, Ischia, Procida, Capri, Stromboli, and Palmaria, have all had their painters and their poets too—but who has ever dreamed of writing upon Maddalena, though *she* may also vaunt herself of her historical recollections? Was she not the Phintonis of the Greeks and Latins? The ruined forts which crown her heights, and whose crumbling walls mingle their grey tints with the masses of granite from which they spring, are still existing witnesses of their importance as a place of refuge, where the population ensconced themselves against the invasion of Turks and pirates; and is not the name of " Nelson " an household word in the mouths of the islanders, who all know that their peaceful Archipelago was once the rendezvous of the fleet of the British hero, and that *there* floated the flag which was so gloriously honoured at Trafalgar by his triumph and his death!

Even at this present moment she is the chosen retirement of an aged man of noble heart and mind, who was the friend of Byron and Shelley, and who has gone thither to seek for health, in an air so pure and an atmosphere so revivifying.

And is it not to the shores of her sister island " Caprera," that the Cincinnatus of our times has withdrawn himself from the world and its delusive hopes, until the day shall dawn on his distracted country, when her people may be found worthy of freedom and capable of attaining it, and he shall be recalled from his plough by the messenger of such glad tidings?

Why is it that Maddalena, whose climate and position offer so many advantages, has never attracted the attention of those wealthy English gentlemen whose beautiful yachts glide " o'er the glad waters of the dark blue sea? " Why is it that the languishing invalid, the misanthrope who has been sated with everything, and the philosopher who is everything to himself, does not come here for health, or for that isolation so congenial both to the strong mind and to the wounded heart? Where can the pallid victim of disease find more examples of health and longevity? Where will the sportsman meet such abundance of game, or the angler hope for better exercise of his art, than in this secluded spot, where the mountains are so picturesque and the blue waters so transparent?

May my present description of this islet prove an attraction to some few travellers, or This was written in 1858. some few invalids, whose presence there may help to decrease the poverty of its inhabitants, extend their little commerce, and make their intercourse with the Continent more frequent! If I should be the means of obtaining for her such advantages as these, my end will be attained and my labour rewarded. CHAPTER I.
"LA MADDALENA."

" And this terrible weather, Madame, does it not frighten you from your projected journey?" was the friendly greeting of Captain D, as, dripping wet from a heavy thunder shower he entered my sitting-room, at no time very light, but now, on a stormy October morning, when the lightning was playing about, and the sluices of heaven seemed to have been opened on the city of Genoa, was so dark that I could scarcely recognize my visitor. I was sitting ready for my departure, and at once replied, " If the sea be not too rough for *you,* Captain, I shall not release you from your engagement."

"Madame," he answered, with a sarcastic smile, " would you compare your courage with that of an old sailor, who has braved danger all his life, and grown grey in the midst of tempests?"

" Certainly not. I never dreamed of such a comparison; but it occurred to me that the father of a family would have a fair excuse for avoiding needless risk."

" It must be allowed, Madame, that we could hardly have been more unfortunate in our weather. The barometer has been falling since yesterday, and, moreover, instead of a passage in the fast-sailing ' St. George,' we shall be tossed about, I know not how long, in the old ' Virgilio,' which backs against the waves. But they say,' what woman wills, God wills;' and since you are determined to go, let us not delay."

I took the arm of my companion, and we left the " Hotel della Vittoria " together.

The aspect of that noisy, bustling part of the city, which extends from the Piazza dell' Annunciata to the bridge, was so changed during this heavy storm, that it was scarcely to be recognized. The eye met neither the young Genoises, gracefully fluttering their fans, nor the matrons enveloped in their variously coloured " mezzara." The ear was not pierced by the shrill cries of the vendors of the " Movi mento," and the multitude of other brochures in public demand. The thunderstorm had sent every one to shelter but that row of women so perseveringly offering their smoking chesnuts for sale. Along the streaming pavement, far or near, nothing was to be seen but one of those files of mules so often traversing the streets of Genoa, heavily laden, but holding their heads high, and shaking their tinkling bells. The Portico Nuovo gave us but a momentary cover from the wind and the torrents of rain, but we soon reached the quay, where we were glad to avail ourselves of one of the common boats. The " Virgilio" was already getting up steam. Although she lay but a short way off, it was not without difficulty that we threaded our way through the multitude of boats which surrounded her. Scarcely had I placed my foot on board, and cast one hurried glance around me, when I could have fancied myself no longer in Europe, but transported to the northern coast of Africa, or to some gulf in the Grecian Archipelago. Never had I witnessed a parallel confusion, never heard sounds more deafening.

I soon discovered that my companion and I A newspaper so called.
were the sole occupants of the chief cabins. In those of the second class there were no passengers at all. In the third, but few. The fourth, however, swarmed with people. This throng was chiefly composed of poor women in tattered clothes, suckling their infants, and closely followed by children of every age, some of them crying, and some consoling themselves with green fruit. Quantities of boxes and cases, sacks of chesnuts, and baskets full of pates de gene, were heaped pell-mell upon the deck, while a mass of spades and pickaxes, and carpenter's tools, completed its multifarious encumbrances.

Already overcome by the weather, I

felt quite discouraged in the midst of such a chaos of miserable objects, whose appearance showed plainly how wild and uncultivated must be the people of the island I was about to visit. I do not know if my impressions are like those of others, but upon *me* the aspect of the sky has so much influence, that a project conceived in a bright sunshine becomes an absolute folly when realized in the midst of cold and rain. I could not help thinking of the " Semillante," the " Castor," and other vessels, much superior to ours, which had nevertheless been lost in the waters we were now to navigate. My disposition to hypochondria went so far as to entail on me a species of remorse at the thought that I was dragging the father of a family into an enterprise which was beginning under such sinister auspices.

However, " Alea jacta erat." The side ladder of the vessel was hauled up, the hatches were closed, the paddle-wheels began to revolve, and in a few minutes the heavily laden " Virgilio " was in the open sea.

I endeavoured to drive away all my sad thoughts, and, in response to a bell which then sounded, I allowed my companion to conduct me into the saloon where breakfast awaited us, and where we found the captain of the vessel, and a Sardinian naval officer charged with the military surveillance of the ship. The destination of the packets on this line is " Porto Torres," the port of Sassari; and it is only once a month that they touch at La Maddalena, in order to land passengers there, some of whom are going to neighbouring islands, and others to the coast of Sardinia.

Our two fellow occupants of the saloon expressed much surprise on hearing that, instead of Porto Torres, I was going to the small island of La Maddalena. It roused their curiosity; and though Captain D related several of his adventures in the Crimea, he could not withdraw their attention from the strangeness of my plan. But I soon found it impossible to take further part either in the conversation or in the repast, for the terrible disorder which no remedy will cure, and against which the efforts of science are powerless, began to seize me so violently, that there was nothing left for me but a sudden retreat from the table. Captain D 's strong arm was scarcely sufficient to support me across the deck, now rocked by the swell. Those who have never witnessed such scenes can form but little idea of them from description. The most exacting of readers would willingly excuse me from the details of all that now met my eye. Let me therefore drop a veil over the picture! During sixteen long hours of unequal struggle, the " Virgilio" had to bear up against the heavy waves of a raging sea. During sixteen long hours was I plunged in that deplorable state, which makes us sensible of all the misery of our nature. At last Captain D entered my cabin with the welcome iutelligence that the worst part of the voyage was over, and that, having reached the Cape of Corsica, we should be sheltered by its mountainous coast.

The promise of so experienced a sailor was realized as quickly as if he had pronounced some magic charm. Everything became calm, as if by enchantment; and after a very tolerable night, I was agreeably surprised in the morning by a bright ray of sun, which presaged a fine day. I dressed myself hastily and went on deck. All my fears vanished, now that my sufferings were over, and that I inhaled the cool air of this radiant morning, and saw the azure-tint of a cloudless heaven reflected in the transparent water below.

All the passengers appeared to enjoy, as I did, this magnificent spectacle, and every face expanded with pleasure at the prospect of a happy and early debarkation. To the east the sea extended without any visible limit, effacing the last faint lines of the Italian coast. To the west we discerned the steep mountains of Corsica, rising in sublime majesty. The declivities which descended towards the shore were covered with a rich and verdant growth, contrasting wonderfully with the masses of granite which formed the foundation of the picture—masses whose jagged tops were partially concealed by fantastically shaped clouds.

It was thus that Corsica first rose to my sight in all its grandeur, displaying its beauties to my eye, and bringing all its glorious recollections to my mind.

The sight was most imposing, and Ihanks to a good telescope, I was enabled to take in all the picturesque details of the coast, along which we passed at a distance of two or three miles. The ground was covered with wood, and plantations of vines and olives succeeding each other without end, and forming on the whole an admirable panorama. At one point the attention was arrested by a chapel, dedicated, perhaps, to the Virgin; at another by a castle of the middle ages. Here some picturesque ruin crowned an eminence, and everywhere the eye discovered some charming perspective, and the imagination carried one beyond the sight; for who can contemplate an unknown country without planting some romance in it, especially if that country be Corsica?

The isles, half lost among the waves, appeared to me like hermits of the sea. Every one of them had a different aspect, a distinctive character, a sort of physiognomy which engraves itself strongly on the memory, and which is seldom seen on the mainland, where the plains are so similar in their uniformity. The isles of the Mediterranean, moreover, have a peculiar and altogether exceptional interest. From our infancy we have been familiar with their names and their histories; and what the books of the student have not taught us, we have afterwards earned from descriptive romances, and some of us by our own travels. The barque of commerce and the tourist-laden packet-boat are crossing incessantly between France and Ausonia's ever classic land, where the inhabitants of the north, tired of their fogs and mists, come to reanimate themselves, and get rid of their melancholy humours.

Corsica enjoys all the advantages of a French Government, but the manners of its natives remind one of the ferocity of past ages, when every man took the law into his own hands. It is remarkable that the nature of the soil and vegetation much resembles the customs of the country. These are obstacles which will long interfere with the progress of civilization. I will not say that little is known about Corsica, but rather that she occupies but little attention. Much more must be done to lift the mysterious veil that covers this country, and which favours the accomplishment of acts quite at variance with the times. The Italy we knew by the descriptions of Goethe appeared to us more poetic than that which we now visit and observe for ourselves, as do our sleeping dreams and waking visions than the objects actually presented to our sight.

For this reason, I suppose, it might be that, fatigued with the bright aspect of the shore, my mind wandered into the interior of the island, under the aged trees of the virgin forests, yet untouched by the woodman's axe, the intricacies of which have served as the refuge of the bandit from the pursuits of justice, and the "vendetta" from their bitter foes.

Venerable Kyrnos! possessing still the woods which were the admiration of antiquity! Seneca knew them, when in his exile he wandered along your shores, and imbibed the inspirations which dictated his "Consolatio ad Helviam.'' Then already the God of War had lit up your shades and trampled down your harvests; when the Ligurians, the Etruscans, the Carthaginians, the Romans, successively invaded your territories, and fought many a sanguinary battle for their possession. Here Belisarius gave combat to the Vandals. Here reigned by turns the Goths, the Lombards, the Francs, the Saracens, succeeded by the Pisans and the Genoises. Although thus often the object of dispute, this island subsequently sank into repose and oblivion, though destined to give birth to the Imperial Eagle, whose thunderbolts lightened the whole world.

My historical reverie was broken by Captain

D, who directed my attention to the little city of Bonifacio, backed by a calcareous rock, which made it very distinguishable. Its construction evinces the strategic talent of the Tuscan Marquis Bonifacio, who gave it his own name, on founding it after his triumphant return from Africa. When we passed it Neptune was kinder to us than usual, and we sailed along a sea of glass. A multitude of islands, far and near, large and small, showed themselves above the limpid waves, through which the course of the " Virgilio " resembled a summer's sail upon a Swiss lake, more than an October voyage through one of the most dangerous passages of the Mediterranean Sea.

Leaving upon our right the granite Isle of Cavallo, we reached one of the group of the Lavezzi, so sadly celebrated by the loss of the " Semillante." This beautiful frigate, laden with munitions of war, and having on board 1000 soldiers and a numerons crew, was wrecked here on her voyage to the Crimea. This inhospitable rock stands like a funeral monument, pointing out the dangers which menace the mariner on his entrance into these straits. Not a single man survived the disaster. A few lifeless bodies were the dumb messengers which told the tale of this frightful catastrophe. Every soldier who goes to the wars, knows that he may be their victim; but it is sad that he should find an obscure grave in the deep, when he thought to die the death of the brave in some glorious struggle on the battlefield.

The island of Santa Maria, which shortly came in sight, was the first object which interrupted these trite reflections. An old lighthouse presides over the flat and sandy shore, recognizable by its yellowish tinge, which distinguishes it from the steep coasts of Razzoli and Budelli.

Leaving behind us the Barrettini, whence the northern point of La Maddalena is just visible, though partly concealed by the Isle of Sparagi, which seems to bar the passage, we entered a bay from which no outlet was visible. We had coasted for half-an-hour the ancient Phintonis, whose perpendicular cliffs rose boldly before us, when the " Virgilio" was veered to the eastward, and traversed the little arm of sea which separates the isle from Sardinia. We then found ourselves in a sort of basin, surrounded by islands. Crowned with forts, St. Stephano lay on our right hand; before us Caprera, backed by the distant mountains of Sardinia, and to our left the smiling coast of La Maddalena, the town of the same name appearing in sight from the roads, and forming a little amphitheatre from the shore. The wheels of the "Virgilio" revolved with less and less velocity, and then stopped altogether, and we were at our destination.

When the reader learns that the only communication between the island and the mainland is by one monthly voyage, he will not be surprised that our arrival was an important event in the eyes of the inhabitants, and that the shore was covered with a crowd of people. If the departure from Genoa was a tumultuous scene, our arrival here greatly surpassed it. The thought of having escaped all the dangers of the sea, and the pleasure of again placing foot upon *terra firma,* in the midst of their relations and friends, diffused a universal joy amongst the passengers. As to the islanders, they set at nought the orders of the Captain, and in spite of the rough opposition of the crew, they tumbled by hundreds over the bulwarks on to the deck; some seeking friends, others goods which they had been long expecting, and some asking political news, and quarrelling for the papers.

My companion had not foreseen this tumult, and the delay it would cause us in landing. To avoid the throng I retired to the after-part of the vessel. As I was watching the little port and the fishing craft at anchor there, Captain D. approached me with an air of pleasure, and pointing to a boat, he exclaimed, " Look, Madam, there is Garibaldi! He will soon be on board! With what joy shall I again clasp the hand of that brave man!"

Notwithstanding the multitude of boats going to and coming from the shore with passengers, I could readily distinguish the General, standing upright, one hand holding a rope. He balanced himself with perfect ease at the prow of his light bark, which was managed by a sailor and a very handsome youth.

The aspect of the man so well known in America and Europe was not strange to me. I had seen him at the time when the eyes of all Italy were fixed upon him. In those days of anxiety and hope—when he came to Rome to defend her from the yoke which menaced her— his appearance then filled me with enthusiasm. Now, it moved me to the bottom of my soul! for since 1849 I had been initiated into all the particulars of his life, and comprehended the real value of such a man; and I may truly say that his noble and serious countenance bore in it the evidence of his always grand and adventurous, and sometimes even tragic, history. I therefore contemplated him, not with the fanatic enthusiasm which idealises its object, but with the consciousness of his actual merits, and the certainty of his being a hero whose self-denial and magnanimity equalled his courage; and my entire attention was concentrated on his figure, from the time he was pointed out to me, until he stepped on deck among the concourse which surrounded him.

Although I had requested Captain D. not to name me to the General till some of the confusion was over, it was scarcely a quarter of an hour before he came to say that Garibaldi desired to be presented to me. We went into the ladies' cabin, and there amidst noise and bustle I exchanged my first words with the illustrious warrior. He inspired me at once with such a feeling of confidence that I seemed to be meeting an old friend; and this arose, no doubt, from the cordiality of his reception aud the sympathy which a fine and sincere character is sure to call forth.

I very soon told him the object of my voyage, in which he alone could assist me; but hearing from him that the documents I wanted were no longer in his possession, I felt much discouraged. However, I could not regret having undertaken my enterprise, as it had accomplished one of the most ardent wishes of my heart. I had become personally acquainted with the man whose great character had occupied my thoughts for many years, and it was with true enjoyment that I heard his opinion of the existing state of Italy, and the critical situation of England in regard to the Indian Mutiny. I was agreeably surprised at the admiration he expressed for my country—the more so, as it is not common to find an oppressed people forming an impartial judgment of a great and free nation.

Garibaldi's eloquence became more and more animated as the conversation proceeded, and more and more captivating as he spoke of the past arid the future of Italy. The fire of patriotism glowed in his lively but earnest face; his open countenance and classic features revealing, in one expressive whole, the goodness and the strength of his character. One could not but perceive what must be the effect of this powerful individuality upon the masses. Such a leader electrifies his troops, in communicating to them, by example, the heroism he feels himself!

" But where, Madame, do you think of taking up your abode V said the General, when Captain

D came to tell us it was now possible to go on shore.

"My friend tells me there is an inn for strangers," replied I, turning to Captain D.

" Certainly, Ma'am, we shall find two rooms at Ruffo's."

"Madame," interrupted the General, "it is quite impossible for you to go into such a place. Let me beg you to come to my house. I regret that I shall not be able to receive you as you deserve, but all I can do is at your service, and I offer it most cordially. Allow me to conduct you to my boat, and before sunset we shall be at my house in Caprera."

The tone in which Garibaldi pronounced these

K words was so persuasive, that I found it difficult to reply by a refusal. I did so, however, being determined to visit La Maddalena, and very unwilling to incommode him. Promising, then, to devote the morrow to a visit to him, he pointed out to me his retreat, situated on the point of Caprera, where the shore, to the east, seemed to shut in the transparent lake on which we were now at anchor. At a short distance from the beach, in a delightful solitude, I discovered a white house, backed by a wall of granite rock.

Three o'clock now struck, Tind it was full time for us to depart; but, before leaving the ship, he advanced towards me with the youth of whom mention has already been made: "You must also know my son Menotti. Some people reproach him with having the air and robust form of a sailor. For myself, I know too well the value of good health, not to encourage him in all manly exercises which strengthen the body, even at the sacrifice, perhaps, of some of that extreme elegance which the world so much delights in!"

I replied, " It seems to me, General, that you have perfectly attained your end, and that your son is endowed with that strength which does not exclude grace," and held out my hand to the young Hercules, whose frank air and noble carriage had already attracted my admiration. Once in the boat, a few strokes of Menotti's vigorous oar brought us to the strand, where we parted with a promise to be early on the morrow at the "Punta della Moneta," the southeastern extremity of La Maddalena, where a very narrow arm of sea separates her from Caprera.

" And what is to become of us, now that we have declined, rather inconsiderately, the hospitality which was so freely offered us?" was the ironic exclamation of my companion, as he followed the porter who carried our luggage through the streets of the mean little town.

" We shall soon know our fate," said I, as our guide turned into a house on the right hand. " A most promising entrance," grumbled my companion, looking up a staircase as straight and almost as steep as a ladder. Some halfnaked children barred our progress. " Whew! what a smell of garlick! enough to make the whole English army draw back!" cried Captain

D, on opening the door of a room where we were encountered by a number of women.

" Have you two rooms to let?" he asked, casting a sceptical glance around the chamber which we now entered, and where we saw an immense bed and an enormous table, round which were seated many of the " Virgilio's" passengers, recruiting themselves after the effects of the sea, by eating, with an excellent appetite, everything that was set before them. The women pushed us into an adjacent closet, saying, " You may lodge there." " But the second room?" asked the Captain, with visible anxiety. " These people are going away again in the steamer, and then you can take their place," was the women's reply, speaking all together.

Our doom was pronounced—we could only resign ourselves to it. The open street was the sole alternative. Our eyes sought in vain even the most indispensable articles of furniture, and always after every glance they rested on the gigantic bed, which was covered with dishes and glasses and tureens, which were almost lost in heaps of boots and shoes and wretched rags of clothing, in which heterogeneous amalgam seemed to be everything for which there was no other place. Nor were live objects wanting. At one corner a poor bitch was suckling her litter; at another a hen sheltered her brood under her wing, and near them a fine pigeon cooed to his mate. What repose could be expected from such a couch, which, no doubt, was also the habitation of other and smaller members of the animal kingdom? I stood stupified and horror-stricken for some moments, and then turned away and followed

Captain D, who said that, since we were condemned to such a fate, we had better at least employ the remaining hours of daylight in seeking our fellow-countrymen whom we intended to visit. Desiring that the rooms should be put into some kind of order while we were away, we obtained a guide to Captain R.'s dwelling, and soon arrived in front of a pretty house, situated at the end of a promontory, about a gunshot from the quay. From my first arrival I had remarked this house, the harmonious lines of its architecture, the colour of its walls, and particularly its fine situation, fronting the sea, and commanding a splendid view on every side.

The loud barking of two large hounds gave notice of the presence of strangers, but the zeal of the two Cerberi was soon quieted by a servant, who asked us to enter. Captain R. came to the door, and said that his dog, " Terrible," did not know what to make of so unaccustomed an event as a visitor, and was rather disposed to give us a " terrible" reception. " His master, however, is more friendly," replied I, as I returned the pressure of the old gentleman's hand, and took the seat to which he led me.

Never did I feel more sensible of the truth of the old saying, that " the friends of our friends are our friends," for, without introduction, or even sufficient excuse, I was intruding on an entire stranger, of whose existence, forty-eight hours ago, I was perfectly ignorant, and yet the mere naming of a mutual friend had produced in a moment something very like intimacy between us.

I gathered from my worthy host's conversation that, after a brilliant career in the British navy, he had visited many places in his own yacht until he had been tempted by the splendid climate, and the great opportunities for hunting and fishing, to establish himself in this island; and here for many years he had now passed a life, divided between the quiet pleasures of reading, and the gentle labours of his vineyard and garden. It cannot be said that solitude weakens and enervates, for a more fresh-spirited and hardy old man I never beheld; and notwithstanding his seventy years, his firm slim figure, the fire of his sharp eyes, and the energy of his every movement, might raise the envy of many a much younger man.

The sight of a fresh heap of newspapers and letters,-which covered the table, made me fear that we had disturbed our host by our unauthorized visit, and we therefore prepared to depart, asking him if he thought we might venture to call upon Mr. and Mrs. C. " Certainly," he replied; " and if you are not afraid of my little boat, it is quite at your service to take you to the Punta della Moneta. It will save you time, and you have not much to lose." With these words he conducted us to the landing-place below, and accompanied by his boatman, Giovanni, we stepped on board the boat.

It was the most beautiful part of the day, when the departing rays of the sun had but a short hour left to gild the valleys with their glow; though even after the moment of setting they would still gladden the highest tops of the mountains, until, bathed in a sea of purple, they abandon the earth to the shadows of night. Never saw I a more translucent sea! never a more resplendent sky, and never in Greece or Italy had I inhaled a milder air! But it is not in the vegetation, the luxuriant meads, or the autumnal tints of the rich woods, that the stranger should find his chief inducement to visit this country. Wherever the eye turns, it rests on gigantic and fantastically formed rocks, whose inhospitable steeps forbid even the use of their scanty herbage, and give the northern stranger an idea of a comfortless desert. But the eye of the poet, and the searching glance of the geologist, will view these majestic masses with the purest delight, whether it be to seek in them the traces of beauty, or the evidences of the God-written annals of nature.

We were now coasting the southern shore of La Maddalena, having on our right the Isle of St. Stephano, until Caprera revealed to our sight all the asperities and the depths of her abrupt declivities, illumined by the roseate reflections of sunset. In about an hour we reached thePunta della Moneta, at the extremity of which stood the white mansion of Mr. C, built in the Moorish style, and we arrived there, after a short walk along a picturesque terrace, where bloomed the cactus and the Indian fig. Giovanni went forward to announce us. Mrs. C is one of those extraordinary women whom England alone can create, and of whom I have found examples in regions the most distant from home. She advanced towards us as far as the door of her romantic habitation, begged us to enter a pretty room even with the terrace, and expressed her regret that her husband was not there to receive us. Mrs. C might be about five-and-forty, still very agreeable in person, and her manners evidenced the distinction of her birth. She had resided here for twenty-five years, and I believe that some catastrophe had condemned her to this voluntary exile. I longed to know the mystery of this destiny, but all I could learn was that she ordinarily accompanied her husband on his long excursions on horseback and in the chase, and even in his fishing voyages—a passion for which they both possessed, to the extent of being several days absent on the open sea.

Mrs. C seemed to penetrate my wishes, but she only gratified them so far as to tell me that by birth she was a lady, by choice a gipsy, and by necessity a farmer's wife. I can only say that her behaviour evinced perfect contentment; and, notwithstanding the complete isolation in which she was placed, without children and without domestics, her life, perhaps, affords more real interest than the existence of some of our queens of fashion, who purchase their triumphs at the cost of so many frivolous but imperious duties. Exclusively devoted to the care of her household and farm, she had formed for herself so extended a circle of activity, that ennui could never reach her. I was told that for seventeen years she had never set foot in the town of La Maddalena. A pleasant fireplace, a choice library, a writing-table covered with books and papers, showed that many calm evenings might be enjoyed in this room. I inquired of Mrs. C the qualities of the small Sardinian horses, and she assured me they deserved the renown they had obtained. " Their price," she said, " never exceeds 200 francs, and their keep is about 150 francs a-year. They require but little care, and can support the greatest fatigue, which I attribute to their breed and their food, composed, like that of the Arabian, of straw and barley. If you will place yourself at the window, I will show you my own miniature charger."

She went out into the garden, and one call of her well-known voice served to bring from his stall the prettiest little horse of dappled grey. He put up his bright eye, and shook his head with a proud but docile air, and followed his mistress, who, having a sieve in her hand, attracted the attention of all the other quadrupeds and all the fowls of the farmyard. Two dogs came out to greet her, wagging their tails. Some pigs, of a kind peculiar to Sardinia, a flight of pigeons, and many fowls with bright red crests, came running to pick up the grains that fell. A bank of laurels, roses, and exotic plants formed the frame of this living picture, the serene beauty of which reminded one of the pastoral manners of the golden age.

Once more in our boat, which glided in its silent course over the waveless water, and the night having by degrees confused every object and every colour in one sombre uniformity, I pleased myself by considering the country life I had just witnessed, and its traces on my mind were more poetic and enchanting than even the reality.

" I do not know," said I to my companion, " what have been the trials to which Mrs. C. has been subjected, but I would accept her past, with all its griefs, if I could at such a price purchase her present happiness." " Particularly this evening," replied the Captain, who was thinking of our return to the inn! " Stop, Giovanni," continued he, as a boat crossed us; "I think that is a fishing boat, and we may perhaps add something to our rather problematical supper."

Such an idea was not at all to be despised; particularly as the fishermen had caught but three red mullets, and we at once secured them for a small coin, which they thankfully took in exchange.

It was late when we entered the town, and on reaching the inn we were disagreeably surprised at finding the large room full of travellers, and the second exactly as we had left it! Captain D. angrily demanded why the rooms had not been prepared and reserved for us. His words seemed rather to confuse the eldest of our hostesses, an old matron, as thin as a spindle, and enveloped in a brown cloak. She asked us, in a dolorous tone, to " pardon her poor daughters, who must have been out of their minds to promise us the second room, as it belonged to an engineer and his family"! At this the Captain's choler became more violent, and his reproaches, mingled with the excuses of the daughters and the protestations of their mother, formed a " crescendo," which soon became a " fortissimo," that almost split the tympanum of our ears.

" Send then for Pietro Susini," said Captain

D, " and he must find us another lodging;" and with this he began to dissect a tough fowl, which he declared must be the progenitor of all the fowls in the place, and, at last, told the old woman to bring some bread, if nothing else was to be had; on which she placed before us some baked paste, as hard as a biscuit, saying, " Our bread is all gone, and there are no bakers here. Every family bakes for itself every Saturday, and when they have no more, they do as well as they can, with chesnuts, or potatoes, or maize."

"Madame," said my friend, smiling, "I warned you that we should have to live like Crusoe in his island." However, our hostess now brought us some fine chesnuts and a straw-covered flask of excellent wine, the first glass of which restored the Captain's equanimity. The women, fearing to lose us, tried all their eloquence to persuade us that one room was enough; but the arrival of Pietro Susini put an end to their entreaties. He told us there were apartments to be had in the house of the sisters Fazio; but, up to the last moment, we had almost a battle to get away. I should have said before, that the Captain had a letter of introduction to Signor Susini, who was one of the authorities of the place. " I am about to take you to some very respectable people," said he, as we entered a house. He opened a door, and we found ourselves in a large apartment, the ceiling of which was formed of canes, interlaced in a pattern. Three women received us courteously. Susini assured us that we should here find a quiet and propriety which was to be met with in few houses in the island. They introduced me into a small chamber, opening out of the vestibule. Here there was a bed, with a damask coverlid and white curtains, a table, and an old prie-Dieu, and the rest of the space was not much more than my trunk required. "There is another room for the Captain," said Susini; " and if you want anything else, you have only to ask for it." " Quite true," said one of the sisters; " everything we have is at your disposal. Our house is small, but our hearts are large! "

The time for tea having arrived, I began to make my preparations, and I presumed that these large-hearted ladies would at least furnish me with some hot water—but no! They allowed me to light my spirit lamp; and instead of offering me any assistance, they only looked on with surprise, and afterwards asked to partake of a beverage which was entirely unknown to them.

After tea Captain D retired to his cell. The sound of his boots as he threw them off, and presently an energetic snore, showed that he had already forgotten his fatigues in sleep. The ladies wished me good night, and left me to the free use of the room, of which I profited to write up my journal.

The consciousness of being thus alone in a strange place, at an hour of universal repose, always awakes in me a peculiar sensation. Fancy is in the ascendant, and runs away with me; and my thoughts not being restrained by any external obstacle, outstrip in rapid flight both time and space.

Having written for a while, I allowed myself to be tempted by the bright moonlight to walk out into the free air, and enjoy the splendour of a night so radiant. The house of the sisters Fazio was situated on the slope of a hill, and at a few steps from the door I obtained an extensive view, illumined by the beams of the beautiful planet. This demi-light, which gives so great a charm to places we love, diffuses a still greater illusion over an unknown country, which our imagination may embellish as it will. The silence of nature was uninterrupted either by the bark of a dog, the cry of an owl, or the noise of the sea waves.

A calm so profound reigned over the sleeping isle, that the most sensitive ear would have failed to distinguish a single sound from any one of the multitude who reposed at this solemn hour on its breast. One might have thought that all life was concentred in the vegetable kingdom, which now filled the air with perfumes the most delicious.

I followed the path which led to the old and abandoned fort of La Guardia Vecchia, until it disappeared amidst a chaos of stones and rubbish. I was afraid of going farther, and I sat me down on a block of granite. The moon was now less brilliant, and some rather ominous clouds appeared at all points of the horizon. The sea, shut in by numerous mountains, isles, and promontories, formed itself into basins of different shapes and extent.

And in all this solitude, thought I, there is so much security, that a whole population is sleeping in peace, with open doors, under the protection of Heaven; and I, a stranger, am wandering about at midnight wherever caprice leads me! I then thought of the wide expanse of sea and land which separated me from my home. Seized, and by degrees absorbed by this impression of solitude, my mind was carried back from age to age, even to the Creation; and the sight of all these islands and mountains awoke in me a vision of that unknown time, when the war of elements overthrew the order of our sphere, making islands rise from the bosom of the deep, and forming seas in the midst of continents.

The probability seems to be that Sardinia was once the centre of all these isles, which no doubt partook her destiny. Let us go back only to what history has chronicled. Sardinia has played but a small political part since the time of Tiberius Gracchus; not because she is insignificant in herself, but because she has had the lot of many men who, endowed with all the gifts of Nature, have been so placed by circumstances as to be unable to develop their qualities, and are thus the victims of that injustice which in all ranks of society exercises an inexorable despotism!

As everything which is concealed has an attraction at once strange and pleasant, I plunged deeper and deeper into thought, and Heaven knows how far I might have gone had not a noise of falling stones aroused me. I turned quickly round, and beheld the tall figure of a man, who, descending the hill, advanced towards me with a firm step.

" Salute," said I to the unknown; who, armed with no weapon more formidable than a walkingstick, inspired me with confidence rather than with fear.

"Salute," replied (according to the custom of the country) the voice of an old man, with an accent so sympathetic, that I determined to profit by the rencontre in finding the shortest way home. Scarcely had the stranger recovered his surprise at my unexpected presence, than he asked what could have caused my being alone in such a place at such an hour.

"Merely," I answered, "that I might contemplate by moonlight the different points of your island! and *you,* an aged man, what could be *your* inducement to leave a comfortable home, and make a nocturnal excursion, so fatiguing as it must be in these mountain paths?"

" Alas! where *is* my comfortable home? " cried the old man, with a sigh. " Look, Signora mia," continued he after a pause, and uncovering his head, displaying his snow-white hair, and turning his majestic figure towards me, " Michele Zicaro can count ninety-eight years, but it is not the weight of age, but of grief and cruel losses, that bears him down."

Touched with compassion at these words, I asked, " Have you no children, no grandchildren, whose affection might soothe your sorrows?"

" I have possessed all, but to lose all, and to pass in misery and bereavement a deplorable old age. The town which now extends itself along the shore, once crowned the hill which still retains the name of Santa Trinita, and where the vestiges of the old buildings may yet be seen. That was the scene of my earliest recollections; there it was that we were kept by fear of the Turks. Half a century and more has since passed over us, but there are even now moments when I can fancy I hear the silver sound of the church bell at daybreak, calling to their work all the inhabitants of the place, for every one felt himself bound to work at the erection of the fort ' Della Camicia,' our only ramparts for the preservation of our goods, and of the honour of our wives, and daughters, and sisters. Every one in the island, not only the young and strong men, but boys and girls, women and aged men, lent a hand to this work of defence, on which our safety so greatly depended. I think I now see this band of voluntary labourers hastening to the place of their appointed work. Yes, Signora, it was a time of fatigue, excitement, and anguish. They called Michele Zicaro the happiest man in La Maddalena; and indeed he really was so, for the pastures of the island did not suffice for his numerous herds, and they were sometimes sent to graze the green meadows of the Barrettini. A worthy circle partook my happiness, in the midst of a group of children who prospered around me. Holy Virgin! shall I never lose the remembrance of that terrible day, which changed all my joys into mourning? It was a beautiful spring morning: we were returning from church, where my eldest daughter had just received the nuptial benediction, and, agreeably with an old custom here, we were descending towards the beach, to finish the *fete* by a marriage feast, with a number of joyous guests. Suddenly as we crossed a ravine we found ourselves surrounded by a horde of pirates, who had just landed. After a vain and useless resistance, for our enemies out-numbered us greatly, and were well armed, I was overthrown with such violence, that I lost my senses, and was unable to see any more. After a while I recovered consciousness, and my ear was struck by the sounds of rage and distress. I comprehended at once all that had passed; my unfortunate companions were standing on the shore in an attitude of despair, pointing to a Turkish galley in the distance, in full sail, laden with women and booty. They were our wives and daughters, the captives of their ravishers."

"All your children! were they *all* taken?" I asked of the old man, whose emotions had forced him to break off his recital.

" There remained to me two sons," he replied, with a sigh, " but they also were soon taken from me. My wounds were scarcely healed when I received the news that the elder of them had perished by shipwreck off the northern coast of Africa! As to the younger, he also would be a sailor. He was deaf to my prayers, and would not take warning by his brother's fate! He persisted in his choice. The British fleet appeared in our waters, and this circumstance awoke the ambition of the lad to such a degree that he could not rest till he had obtained a berth in the Admiral's own ship. The moment of his departure is always before my eyes! I think I again receive the last adieu of my darling boy, my last and only hope! He was radiant with joy, speaking only of success and speedy return! He embraced me tenderly, and tried to console me, but I was sad and downcast, and foresaw a further misfortune! Penetrated with this presentiment, I stood watching the disappearance of the last sail of this splendid squadron, whose presence here had brought back security to our coasts. The brilliant victory over the French and Spanish fleets which was purchased by the death of the British hero deprived the poor Zicaro of his last child! My boy fell in the battle of Trafalgar!"

" He partook, then, of the fate of Nelson."

"Yes, Signora; you have named the great man whose example enchanted my son; and what a man he was! He first showed his genius at Aboukir, and, like a meteor, he arose in the East,'and after a rapid career he sank, like the sun, in splendour, in the West."

" Did you know the Admiral personally?"

" I not only knew him well, but loved him well," replied the old man, with a proud air. " No one could approach him but with respect amounting almost to reverence! Every time he set foot on our shore, he remained some time with us, and with the kindness inherent in his nature he questioned us all of our families and affairs. Often did he mount the hills that looked over the sea, and as he enjoyed the charming prospect, he made me recount to him the incidents of my life, and the history of our little isle. The church of La Maddalena possesses a souvenir of his generosity, in two fine candelabra and a chalice of silver. When he took leave of us, he promised that, if he returned victorious from the battle he projected, he would make the island a present equal in value to a well laden brigantine. Ah, Signora, let me assure you, it is not the loss of this rich gift that I regret—what I deplore is the premature death of so great a man, and of my poor boy r

" Zicaro, at that epoch you were in the full power of manhood, and did you not again marry V

" Ah, Signora, I did; and during that second marriage I saw a new spring time around me, till that terrible malady, which you also must know well, decimated our population, and deprived me of wife and children at once."

" Indeed! and was the cholera so violent here?" "Alas, yes; and no sooner did it appear than all our physicians abandoned us to our fate. The sick and the dying were deprived of all help, and those who escaped the disease had to support the pangs of hunger afterwards, for the authorities of the town interdicted the importation of everything. Those who had not the means of escaping to Sardinia must have died of famine, had not the Government interfered and taken measures to supply us with food. In a few days we celebrate the anniversary of the dead —a day consecrated by the Church to a visit to the tombs, which we then garland with fresh flowers every year. I am now descending from the cemetery, where I have been to prepare it for this ceremony. In that sad place, where all my happiness lies buried, I have passed a great part of the night, absorbed in grief, and in the recapitulation of my successive bereavements."

This recital threw me into rather a sad meditation. " So then," thought I, " this small spot of earth, little known and less visited, has not escaped the vicissitudes of fate. Its shores, in appearance so tranquil, have been the theatre of many sanguinary invasions. Its people have been the victims of disease. They have endured famine, and here, as everywhere else, the passions have had their sway. The echoes of European wars have reverberated from these rocks, and the memory of the naval hero of England lives in the hearts of these islanders, mingled with gratitude for the benefits he conferred on them. And yet their annals have still to be written, and no bard has yet sung them. All that has escaped oblivion, lives only in the excited brain and the broken heart of a poor nonagenarian, who must himself soon pass away and his recollections be buried in his grave.

Such were my thoughts as I again crossed the threshold of the house and sought my chamber.

If my rencontre with Zicaro had not been enough to banish sleep, my surroundings would have sufficed. A simple cloth curtain separated my room from the bed of the three ladies, so that I was the compulsory auditor of a sleeping monologue from one, the constant snoring of the second, and the asthmatic cough of the third, and all these sounds were mixed with the clucking of the fowls which shared their apartment. But the noise which troubled me most was the patter of a shower of rain, which threatened to spoil our morrow's excursion to Caprera. I listened to it with some anxiety, as it sometimes seemed to diminish and then again increase, until I heard distinctly the footsteps of somebody in the vestibule, who appeared to be groping in the dark for something he could not find. Suddenly there was a violent crash, accompanied by a cry of alarm, which made me jump.

" Gracious heavens!" cried all the women at once, "what can have happened?" " *What* can have happened?" re-echoed a voice which I immediately recognised, " come here and see, and help me out."

" The Captain is all in the cellar," exclaimed the youngest of the three. " Only *half*" answered my lively friend; " the superior half is still in air, though the inferior hangs in vacuo."

During this short colloquy the women had struck a light, and put on in haste a few indispensable garments, before they ran to his rescue. I should not have been a woman had I not given way to my curiosity, and I peeped through my half-opened door to ascertain with my own eyes what had occurred. In spite of the real interest I felt in his mishap, I found it impossible to resist a loud fit of laughter when I saw the three sisters, in most fantastic costumes, using all their endeavours to release their guest from the trap in which he was caught.

" In the name of all the saints!" said he, " one might as well live in the time of Don Quixote and the knights-errant, if one cannot cross the room in search of one's travelling-bag without falling into an ambush! Wishing to get at my coffee to prepare it for the morning, the floor gave way, and I fell "

" Only into the cellar!" interrupted the women.

" Only!" replied he. " Well, thank heaven, I am no worse off than the Holy Father himself was when he visited the Convent of St. Agnes." With which words he disappeared into his cell.

I afterwards found that his allusion was to a story of the Pope and his attendant dignitaries having been precipitated through the floor of the refectory of a convent when they were feasted by the monks, without any more disastrous consequences than attended the captain's fall.

CHAPTER II. THE ISLAND OF CAPRERA AND ITS CINCINNATUS.

The rain had scarcely ceased. The dull sky, still covered with clouds, lay heavy on the horizon, when, determined to brave the weather, and equipped accordingly, we quitted our lodging at eight o'clock in the morning.

" The roads are in too bad a condition to allow you to go by land to the Punta della Moneta," said our cicerone Susini, " and therefore I have bespoken Maestro Giulio's boat to carry you direct to Caprera, and he will himself take charge of it."

The thick mud which covered the few streets we had to pass through to the shore completely justified Susini's words. We therefore gladly availed ourselves of his plan, and on the beach we saw Giulio's boat preparing for our reception. As we walked down, I said to Susini, "I see that you will never want materials for your houses, since you build them of the very granite on which you lay their foundations;" for I observed that a new building was rising on the rock, out of which the masons were at the same time quarrying stones for its walls.

" Most of these islands," he replied, " are immense quarries of granite, but it varies much in quality and value. That of this island is inferior, but some of them produce a kind which is rich in spar, and has a roseate tinge, and may be compared with any that comes from Egypt. The isle' Dei Cavalli,' which you passed on your voyage, is celebrated for its ancient Roman quarries, where were found, as also at Testa, in Sardinia, some columns shaped out in the rough, and others nearly finished. We know from history that the Pisans took from the peninsula of Testa the columns of their church of San Giovanni, and it is very probable that the peristyle of the Pantheon came from the same source."

The arrival of Maestro Giulio interrupted our conversation. He came to tell us that the boat was quite ready, and we took our places in it at once, together with his nephew and three sons all with fowling-pieces in their hands and dogs at their side, and all going over to Caprera for a day's sport. Susini, wishing us a good voyage, promised to meet us in the evening at the

Punta della Moneta.

"What boat is that, tacking across the strait?" asked Captain D.

" It must be the General's," said Giulio.

" You are right," replied the Captain, " for he promised to meet us at nine o'clock, and there, no doubt, he is, with his accustomed punctuality."

A long distance, however, lay between us and the white sail that had attracted the sharp eye of my companion, and I had time and leisure enough for observing the capricious forms of the rocks as we rowed by them. On the Sardinian coast, just opposite La Maddalena, there was one which particularly amused me. It was called " Capo del' Orso," for on its top was a block of stone that precisely resembled a bear sitting on its haunches. When we consider that this cape has the same name in the geography of Ptolemy, we must conclude that its form was the same 2000 years ago; and as it must be the action of the atmosphere which in the course of many centuries has sculptured these solid rocks into the forms they bear, the origin of these curious similitudes is lost in the dark night of time.

While the sight of scenery so new to me was thus delighting my mind, the boat we had seen at a distance had been gradually approaching us, and we were very soon able to distinguish the General sitting at the helm. Shortly afterwards we were near enough to exchange salutations. " I think," said Captain D, " that we shall do best by remaining in Giulio's boat, for the wind is high, and it is always difficult to change when there is much sea." " There is not so much as to oblige us to refuse the General's civility," replied I; and in a few minutes we had stepped from our poor skiff into the General's beautiful bark; and when I expressed my regret that he should lose so much of his precious time, he replied, with naive grace, "There will only be one workman less at my house to-day, and such a visit as yours is a pleasant excuse for a holiday. I now only wage war with stone, and see," showing his labour-roughened hand, " if a day's rest is not desirable for the poor builder!"

After a short run, the swift boat entered a little harbour, formed by nature; and crossing in a few paces the beach, we trod the odoriferous soil and the green close sward of Caprera.

But how different from her sister island! No picturesque fishing boat gives life to her waters—no pleasant little spot appears along her shores—no ruined forts crown her heights —but one mountain chain upon another raises its rugged masses in amphitheatric form before the wondering eye of the stranger All that surrounds him here is severe and vast, as if Nature had purposely designed it for the residence of the Cincinnatus of our day! The mastic and the arbutus, the myrtle and the heath, and a number of aromatic plants, group themselves among the rocks and over the turf on which, in ascents more or less steep, you walk from the sea to the habitation of Garibaldi.

A short half-hour brought us to the enclosure of flower-beds which extends along the front of the house. Several dogs ran out to welcome their master with the violent expression of their joy, and to be rewarded by his caresses.

" Those must be the ruins of your first dwelling," said I, pointing to a fallen log house.

" Of my second," he replied. " My first was a simple sail, of which I made a tent; but if you will permit me, I will now conduct you into my third, which I have built of more durable materials. It has, as you see, but one storey, and I have copied the style of the South American villas, and covered it with a flat roof, which forms a terrace walk."

The beautiful appearance of this mode of construction is extremely agreeable to the eye; and, on entering the house, I found that the interior corresponded in character with the facade—a praise which cannot always be awarded to our modern fabrics. Every room was ample and well ventilated. The harmony of their proportions proved that the architect thought more of producing becoming apartments than of submitting to the mere rules of his art.

In a room which had been occupied by one of the two friends who shared the General's rural life, I observed a little collection of the flags of several nations; and, on inquiring the meaning of these souvenirs of war, he seemed anxious to avoid a reply, and presently left the room, for he is not one of those who are the recounters of their own successes.

These flags, which I now examined more attentively, were the trophies of his triumphs, and recalled many a brilliant episode in his heroic career. I fixed my eye upon the standard of Monte Video, presented to her brave defender after the battle of St. Antonio. It was on the 8th July, 1846—a memorable day —on which Garibaldi, at the head of 200 Italians, found himself surrounded "by troops, consisting of 1200 men, under the command of General Gomez. Instead of standing on the defensive, which, under like circumstances, no chief could have been blamed for doing, he attacked, with his handful of followers, this force so greatly superior in number, and after a conflict of five hours, Gomez, with his infantry in disorder, and his cavalry in confusion, abandoned the field to its conqueror!

The contemplation of this flag brought also to my mind Alexander Dumas's little work of " Monte Video, ou la nouvelle Troye," in which he renders such transcendent justice to its dauntless defender, proclaiming with enthusiasm his superiority as a warrior and a man! The facts related in that book are, as Garibaldi himself allows, quite true; but it seems that the praises lavished on him appeared to him excessive, and he was thus prevented from thanking its author for his work.

Having gone over the house, the General invited us to take some refreshment; but we had so little time, and I was so anxious to walk over his grounds, that I proposed starting at once on this expedition. "At least," said he, " let me introduce you first to my daughter Teresa," and he left the room in search of her. I threw a rapid glance over his library. To my mind a man's library is the best index to the character of him who formed it; for books are not like unwelcome visitors—they do not come unbidden, and only surround those who seek them and love them. This little collection was composed chiefly of works as solid as their possessor, whom they have followed to the wild shores of Caprera, to charm his short intervals of leisure. Side by side with the best treatises on the art of war and navigation, I saw the names of Shakspeare, Byron, and Young; farther on were the most esteemed works on natural philosophy and science, the "Cosmos" of the great German thinker, the Ethicks of Plutarch, the Discourses of Bossuet, and the delightful Fables of La Fontaine, which conceal so much of the profound under the disguise of naivete.

The entrance of the youthful Teresa ended my literary review. I saluted with much interest this beautiful girl, in whose regular features I recognized the traces of her father's countenance, while the flexible firmness of their movements reminded me of the Brazilian origin of her mother. Never did a complexion of golden brown so harmonize with light-coloured hair. Was it the softness of her dark chesnut coloured eye, or the expression of a physiognomy which at one time betrayed the petulance of a child, and at another the timidity of a young maiden, which gave so great a charm to her entire person? In honour of our visit, she had assumed a "toilette extraordinaire," but I would rather have seen her in her usual costume, with the sling which she uses so adroitly thrown over her shoulder. Curious, that this oldest of instruments of war and the chase should still retain its position in this kingdom, and that the form of the Sardinian "Fionda" should be so identical with that which David used in his combat with Goliath!

We now began our tour of the grounds, which was an enterprise of some hours, of which the pleasure surpassed the fatigue; for the survey of this large estate, just brought into cultivation, and the judicious explanations of our guide, so eminent in everything he undertakes, were as interesting as they were instructive,

It was in the month of May, 1855, that Garibaldi landed for the first time in Caprera, which at that period might have been described as a mass of granite, clothed here and there with a thin crust of earth, which was in part so covered with loose stones, that it produced little beyond a few brambles and a scanty supply of aromatic plants; now, at the expiration of but two years and a half (when I was there) may be seen a fine house and garden, and a large space in cultivation, entirely surrounded by a "muro a secco," a mode of building much resorted to in Tuscany and other small Italian States, with this difference, however, that whereas all which I had before seen were merely rough stones placed one on another, the wall around this domain, though equally without mortar, was built of blocks which had been squared and dressed by the tool. Garibaldi told me that he had done much of this work with his own hands, but that other necessary employments obliged him to give it up.

This enclosure comprehends within its limits a nursery of cypress and chesnut trees, figs and other fruit trees, and a garden of vegetables, vines, and even sugar canes. Everything flourishes under this magnificent sky and fertilizing sun. Pools of Mater, fed by natural springs, are distributed here and there, thus maintaining a sufficiency of moisture, which, united with the sun's heat, quickens the development of vegetation.

Several kilns were burning into charcoal the roots of shrubs that had been cleared off the ground. But while every freshly ploughed slope, where so lately the bush and the stone had reigned supreme, promised a rich harvest, every now faint, now louder, bark of a dog, and every echoing shot, warned the poor birds on the berry-laden boughs that they could no longer enjoy their lives in safety.

If the survey of this young and promising possession afforded us so much gratification, the conversation that passed at dinner gave us no less pleasure. We spoke chiefly in Italian, but from time to time the General expressed himself in French, with that rare perfection so difficult to attain. His sonorous voice, full of power and sweetness, called to mind the dominant qualities of his character; and if his eloquent language was not seasoned with wit, it was always full of knowledge and enthusiasm, and such as is seldom to be met with in a man of action.

When a few years ago I read Hoffstetter's Journal of the Campaign in Italy ("Hoffstetter's Tagebuch aus Italien"), a work which gives a faithful picture of the events of 1849, and also contains many interesting particulars of the public and private life of Garibaldi, I was far from thinking of even the possibility of being the recipient of the hospitality of this eminent man, whose deeds then awoke all my sympathy. Our conversation turned naturally on the past. Acquainted as I was with the disastrous events which caused the death of his wife, I did not dare to pronounce her name, but the General himself led the way to it. It seemed to please him that all the occasions on which the Brazilian Amazon had displayed her courage and presence of mind were so fresh in my memory, and with the same animation which so often lighted up his countenance when his beloved country was his theme, he now spoke with tearful eye and tremulous voice of the heroine of Imbiturba, Morroda Barra, Caquari and Lages.

But it was not alone of her heroic qualities that he spoke. The womanly virtues of the never-to-be-forgotten Anita, he recounted with proud acknowledgment. Her sacrifices as a wife and a mother, the excellence of her heart, and the affability of her manners, he scarcely knew how to praise enough, at the same time holding her up to his daughter as a pattern and example.

In the year 1849 I was witness of the enthusiasm which he raised when he hastened to the rescue of the Eternal City from a disgraceful yoke; and if that excited outbreak, those thundering "evvivas" found then an echo in my heart, the veneration which I now feel for the Liberator must of course be doubly intense and true. No elegant American cloak now hangs on his shoulders. No ostrich-feather flutters proudly from his helmet. No picturesque-clad Moor follows his charger. No devoted companions obey his nod! In plain and humble civil attire, with but two faithful friends to share the leisure of his rocky isle, the cultivation of a waste is the object of his industry, the education of two dear children his recreation!

But it is not desponding hopelessness, it is not petty irritation, that has placed him in voluntary exile and apparent oblivion. The same heroism, the same hope, the same love of country still fill his heart, and bright years will yet open upon his future life! But exactly because the purest motives impel him, the most honourable intentions are his incitement, he prefers rather to wait in self-denying patience, than to prostitute his abilities to the satisfaction of a lust for renown, or an ambitious self-love.

After dinner, as we prepared to leave the house again, the weather looked uncertain; a fresh breeze had sprung up which now collected the clouds into masses, and now again dispersed them; letting a ray of sunshine through their openings, to light up the picture before us. Several small horses were feeding quietly, and giving life to the green meadow; goats grouped themselves on the most acute peaks, and stood out in relief against the sky, remaining in perfect immobility till Teresa surprised them by a stone which whistled through the air from her sling, when they bounded down, scampered over the even ground, and disappeared.

Wishing to have a view of the whole panorama of the island, I undertook, under the guidance of Garibaldi's two friends, the ascent of the Tejalone; but after climbing up for above an hour, we encountered some blocks of stone, almost inaccessible, and thickets of brambles quite impervious. The summit, which I thought so easily attainable, now appeared more distant every step we took, and I was obliged to renounce my project. The same path downwards was so much more difficult than before, that we were necessitated to choose another, by which we obtained a view of a different side of the island.

Although Caprera is five miles in length, and fifteen in circumference, and a large proportion of it capable of cultivation, there are at present but six proprietors—the General, Mr. C. of Maddalena, and four shepherds. The first is the only one who possesses a house; Mr. C. purposes building one; but the shepherds live in some of the natural caves among the rocks. I was conducted to the mouth of one of these grottos, and there we found Maestro Giulio and his sons, who had finished their sport, and were talking with a shepherd and some other huntsmen.

" Have you killed much to-day?" asked one of my companions.

" Only two boars," was the reply. " The bad weather diminishes the ardour, and spoils the scent of the dogs."

" And these boars, to whom do they belong?"

' What!" cried I, " has the game proprietors *here* also? and how are the hunters to know whom it belongs to?"

" In this island, Madam, as in many parts of Sardinia and Corsica, the boars we hunt are but a race escaped from the domesticated swine; and as soon as a proprietor sees a wild sow with a litter by her side, he marks them in a particular way which lasts till their death, and thus they become his property."

We continued in conversation on this curious subject till we reached the house, without thinking how late it was, although the twilight already gave us a warning to depart. The wind had much increased, and our brave host declared that he must take us back himself; and he and his son, and one of his friends, prepared themselves accordingly.

The waters of the Archipelago, at times as tranquil as a lake, were now much agitated. The wind whistled with fury, and made our light canoe fly before it over the frothing waves.

Menotti executed with rapidity and precision the directions of his father, and his friend and Captain D managed the sails. Fear was impossible when with such men as these, but still I will confess that I was not sorry when our keel grated on the shore. Mrs. C, who had been watching our rough passage from her window, came down to us and invited us into her house, A bottle of wine of her own growth was not a thing to be despised; we took leave of the General and his companions, who went off in their boat again. I know not what we should have done without Susini, who was punctual to his appointment, to guide us home.

It was one of those nights which the immortal poet of the " Inferno " calls " una povera notte," and we were obliged to grope our way over an uneven road, along which we were sometimes driven on by the wind, and sometimes deluged by the rain, the squalls succeeding each other almost without cessation.

We had scarcely attained the half of our distance when we distinguished other footsteps than our own, and my ears were startled by hearing my own name pronounced in an unknown voice, and who should it be but Mr.

C, returning home, leading his horse by the bridle!

In spite of my desire to stop and speak to the eccentric inhabitant of the " Punta della Moneta," we could in so terrible a night only exchange a word and an English shake of the hand, and even that was much for people so tired, and wetted, and blown to pieces as we were. At last after a two hours' walk we reached our lodging once more.

I soon forgot my fatigues and the contrarieties of our nocturnal promenade, for before I had completed the exchange of my dripping garments for dry ones, a visit from Captain R was announced.

The conversation of such a man, so full of sense and imagination, charmed me the more as he expressed a lively interest in Italy and a love for the fine arts, which soon produced that sort of mutual understanding which always exists between persons of similar tastes. The intimacy of Captain R. with Byron and Shelley had left in his mind a store of precious recollections. He told me the details of the passion which Byron had conceived for the fair Guiccioli. He spoke of his enthusiasm in the cause of freedom, of his generous conduct towards the conspirators of the Romagna, where his name is still held in public veneration, for he knew how to excite admiration by his character as well as by his genius. He told me also of the profound mosphere. In the centre of such a scene rose the bright flame which was reducing to ashes the bodies of our two friends. The smoke enveloped the cross for a moment, and then mounted high towards heaven,.like a symbol of Christian faith and the immortality of the soul.

"The heart of the Poet had been removed, and was subsequently buried with his ashes in the Protestant cemetery at Rome.

" It was thus that England lost one of those men of genius who promised to add to her glories. Nobody denies Shelley's great fault. It is difficult to defend him; but it should not be forgotten that after his marriage had conferred on him more happiness of mind, his irritation against mankind became less bitter. He had begun to rectify his opinions, and we may find in this some justification for a belief that had he lived longer, he would have completely abandoned his errors, and his genius would have shone forth without a blemish."

Such was the narration of Captain R. , and it had carried us, unconsciously, deep into the night. Our fading lamp brought with it the evidence of the lateness of the hour. He seemed pleased with the opportunity of recalling his recollections in the presence of one who so evidently sympathised with him. He retired with a pressing invitation to me to partake of an " Anchorite's repast" with him the next day.

M CHAPTER III.

A DAY AT LA MADDALENA.

" Des que l'Auror en son char remontrait,
Un miserable Coq a point nomine chantait,
Aussitot notre vieille, encore plus miserable,
S'affablait d'un jupon crasseux et detestable,
Allumait une lampe, et courait droit au lit,
Oii de tout leur pouvoir, de tout leur appetit,
Dormaient lcs deux pauvres servantes."
La Fontaine.

From my infancy the programme of my daily duties included the study of one of the Fables of La Fontaine, and if ever these first troubles of my early life came back vividly to my mind, it was in the house of the sisters Fazio. I believe I have already said that my companion and my hostesses retired in good time to their beds. As soon as they were gone I began my writing, and about the time when I was attaining my best sleep, " nos vieilles s'affablaient d'un jupon crasseux et detestable," and began their household arrangements for the day. They had found out that the " fils de la maison " had once served under Captain D, and in consequence of this discovery their friendship for the gallant seaman almost amounted to a passion. It showed itself most at the matutinal hours when he made his early appearance. They overwhelmed him with attentions, and questions, and exclamations, so that I could well say with the poor Marguarite, Meine ruhe ist bin "! though, thank God, *my* heart was not oppressed; and I took some pleasure in overhearing these conversations in the Genois dialect, as they were cutting bread and warming coffee for their breakfast.

The crow of the cock this morning awoke us to a splendid day. The night's rain had exhausted all the clouds, and the sun had warmed the balmy air around us. It was one of those fair autumnal mornings only to be seen in Italy, and which make us dream of spring-time. At eight o'clock Susini knocked at the door, to take us to his little cottage to breakfast.

The order and propriety, so rare in Italy, seemed to be equally so at La Maddalena (of course, I always except the Den of Ruffo!) I was surprised on entering Susini's sitting room, paved with brick, and with whitewashed walls, to find there a Broadwood's piano, contrasting with a furniture otherwise perfectly Spartan. He told me, however, that his sister had married an Englishman, who, after the death of bis wife, had quitted the island, but left this instrument behind him.

Although wretchedly in want of the tuner's hammer, I was entreated to sit down to it; but, luckily, the entrance of a young couple allowed me to rise again without having committed much sacrilege against harmony.

Susiui presented us, with apparent pride as well as pleasure, to bis daughter, about fifteen years old, married a few months since to Augusto Fortuna. This young man, who had been an active performer in the events of 1849, had been obliged to fly his country on the entrance of the French into Rome. A fortunate chance conducted him to La Maddalena, where, since his marriage, he has become in a measure naturalised. In him was visible the prototype of that handsome and sombre countenance which one meets in the Corso at the hours of "La Passeggiata;" while his youthful wife, fair, fresh, and delicate, might be compared with truth to an opening rose. The husband was an " elegant." He wore varnished boots. His cravat had the last new tie, his handkerchief the last new scent, and his hands were covered with kid gloves of the last new colour. As to the lady, the circumference of her crinoline, the number of her flounces, the beauty of her lace, and the cut of her magnificent silk robe; in short, everything in her toilette, was in such exact conformity with the fashion, that she might have walked into any saloon in Paris without exciting the least surprise, except by her beauty. To look at the blocks of rough rock, and the fishing huts of this little island, who would have imagined that even here also reigned, in all its tyranny, that irresistible power which we call " La Mode?"

" What shall we do now?" said Susini, as we rose from breakfast. " Would you like to ascend the heights of 'LaTrinita' and 'Guardia Vecchia,' or would you prefer a visit to Captain R or Mr. Webber?"

" I hope," said I, " that with your guidance we shall be able to make the entire tour of the island; but, before everything, let us go and inquire after Captain R, who has sent me word that he has been taken ill in the night, and cannot receive us to-day at dinner."

" I fear our dear friend has been attacked by one of those violent palpitations of the heart to which he is too subject," said Susini. "They have, however, become less frequent of late, and it is to be hoped that our climate will free him from them entirely."

We soon arrived at his dwelling. His altered look showed the seriousness of his illness. Sorry at being deprived of our company at dinner, he invited us to come back at the hour of tea, and by his advice we deferred the ascent of " La Trinita" till the evening, in order to see the sunset from its summit.

He offered us his boat to take us to the farm. The day was so fine that it might be said to have presented the charms of all the fine seasons at once. The breath of spring was blowing beneath the sky of summer, and the heavens had the transparency and the magic colours of autumn. Our skiff glided lightly along the flowing bank, and I thought myself under the fascination of an enchanting dream. A delicious feeling of silence and solitude came over me as I placed my foot on the smiling and desert shore.

What is there that has a more exalting and inspiring effect on the mind than solitude and an intimate acquaintance with uncontaminated nature? Justly was man created for society. Well may the bustle of life be the best school of character, the best battle-field of virtue; but I venture to assert that, as the sapling is stunted in its growth by being too thickly planted, the noblest qualities of man must suffer a like restriction by a ceaseless contact with his fellows. I think that it would tend to decrease the tedium of life if, instead of shunning solitude, we should accustom ourselves to it as one of the first duties of self-education, and seek, in obtaining knowledge of ourselves and of nature, those imperishable treasures which are so indispensable in the strife of the world, but so seldom attained.

With what delight did I walk along this smooth plain, now pressing beneath my feet a velvety turf, and now a track of fine sand glistening in the sun! Here ran quickly over the ground a pretty beetle, with wings shining like metal; and there a multitude of lizards wagging their tails, and proving that even in November one was still under the influence of summer.

Do not look here for the beauties of the " Isola Bella," or the " Isola Madre," so admired by the timid tourist who dares not pass the " Lago Maggiore," the general boundary of his travels, and who seems to think that Italy is a mere nest of brigands, forgetting that the papers daily tell of murders and robberies in the centre of populous cities, more frequent and more horrible than ever occurred in the places he fears to visit. The beauties here are of a different kind!

Neither will you see any iron gates, adorned with proud armorial shields— nor have to wait till an over-fed porter chooses to answer your summons. Here you are not placed under the supervision of a series of custodiers, until at last you are delivered up to the gardener, to listen to his unintelligible catalogue of exotics. Here there is nothing of the kind; you are in Captain

N 's grounds before you are aware of it, for a low " muro a secco" will scarcely have arrested your attention, and there is no other protection. Pluck as many flowers as you will, for there is no Argus-eyed watchman to forbid you. To nature and to nature only is entrusted the forming, the nourishing, and the protection of this natural garden.

I will not fall into the same mistake for which I have been reproaching the gardeners of the great, and I therefore abstain from any catalogue of the plants which flourish in this little corner, so well protected and so sunny; but we may find there all the gifts of Flora and Pomona, from the common heath to the tropical palm, from the mastic to the vine, from the cabbage to the sugar cane.

Mr. Webber's house, to which we next bent our steps, is situated about a mile from the shore, and forms, with its surrounding grounds, an object sufficiently imposing to produce a desire to view it more nearly. We approached it by a newly-formed carriage drive. The power of riches displayed itself on all sides; and if La Maddalena had but a few more such wealthy colonists, to whom money makes everything easy, the dreamy solitude of the island would quickly be replaced by noise and bustle. The greatest activity prevailed without and within. Troops of labourers worked in the plantations

M 3 and in the buildings. Several grooms were dressing the shining coats of spirited horses, while other servants were opening cases of elegant furniture. The rooms were full of Genoese artificers, laying variegated parquets and pavements. The noise of their hammers kept time with their songs. Some were whistling and some talking, and yet all so entirely devoted to their employments, that it was difficult to find any one to announce our arrival. We were introduced into a room *encumbered* with works of art, pictures in magnificent frames, and books in resplendent bindings; and in the midst of all this, we could not but perceive that our visit, though politely received, was singularly inopportune. Mr. Webber was quite preoccupied with all his treasures, and with the appointment of Vice-Consul, of which he had just received the official announcement.

I afterwards heard that the new Vice-Consul had made a large fortune in Australia, where he had passed ten years in making and selling hats, a circumstance which decreased my wonder at his having, in the pride of his riches, displayed all the magnificence of cities in the rural plains of a remote island like this. The building was of a kind of Moresque-Italian style, and well placed in an amphitheatre of hills.

Having partaken with Susini of the modest repast the sisters Fazio had prepared for us, and renewed our strength with a few glasses of excellent wine, we commenced our walk to La Trinita. The road wound gradually up a gentle ascent, now covered with brambles, and now with stones. From time to time we encountered processions of women and girls, telling their beads devoutly, as they returned from their pilgrimage to the chapel of La Trinita, accompanied by children laden with boughs of arbutus. Here and there were seen horses and cows, and goats wandering at pleasure. A walk of an hour-and-a-half brought us to the most elevated point of the island. I do not remember ever to have derived so much gratification at so little trouble. The incomparable clearness of the atmosphere, united with the golden tints of an autumnal sunset, permitted us to trace the delicate outlines of the most distant mountains. From such an elevation, and by some optical illusion, the isles and promontories between La Maddalena and the Sardinian coasts formed in appearance six lakes.

In no book, ancient or modern, have I ever found any description of La Maddalena. Mons. Mimault, Consul de France in Sardinia, where he resided many years, is the only author who has ever mentioned it. In speaking of the district of Terra Nova, he says— "The isles in the Straits of Bonifacio are considered the third district of the province of Gallera. The most considerable of them is La Maddalena, the ancient Phintonis of the Greeks and Latins, having a superficies of sixteen square miles. Caprera has but eight, and San Stephano five. The others, Santa Maria, Razzoli, Budelli, Sparage, are hardly to be called inhabited, as they only contain a few rude huts for the shelter of the shepherds when they go to look after the flocks of the farmers of La Maddalena. In this isle, at a point called "Calagavela," a little community exists, composed of settlers from Corsica, in number about 1500. They are celebrated for their active and This was written in 1825. Their number now exceeds 2000. The name of "Calagavela" exists no longer; at least I never heard it used by any one.
laborious habits, and also for their gaiety of disposition. They are all more or less sailors, and engage in the navy and the mercantile marine of Sardinia."

The church of Santa Trinita, protected by the highest rock in the island, is the only building still standing entire amongst the scattered ruins on the mountain. This temple, in all its primitive simplicity, has something touching about it. Its walls are covered with a multiplicity of "Ex votos" and pictures, representing the miraculous deliverances of the faithful from shipwrecks and other calamities. Once a year, at a certain fete, a priest says mass in this rustic fane, the doors of which are open day and night. The order and propriety which reign within, the freshly-culled flowers which deck its altar, prove with what zeal the islanders visit this shrine.

Gladly would I have lingered longer on the romantic site of this lonely church, had not the approach of twilight warned us that we must make the best of our way to Captain R.'s. After this long day of walking and fatigues of all sorts, the sight of his well-spread tea-table was a refreshing one. Nothing was wanting to complete the comforts which an Englishman knows so well how to gather round him wherever he establishes himself, and we enjoyed it all with double zest, when we saw that the indisposition of our host had passed away, and that he entered with all the energy of his amiable nature into a conversation remarkable in many respects.

After giving us some very interesting particulars of his military life, and of his long voyages, he took from his little bookcase two documents, which must now be looked upon as rarities beyond price. One was the identical journal which his father kept when mate on board Captain Cook's ship, on the last voyage of that great navigator round the world. The other was a very exact and minute chart of that voyage.

"Our Government," said Captain R. , " had made an unsuccessful attempt at exploring the North Pole. A high reward was offered by Act of Parliament for the discovery of the passage supposed to exist between the two seas. In 1776 Captain Cook undertook the expedition in the sloop 'Resolution,' and my father went as mate. He was very skilful in measuring distances and in making charts.'

Here Captain R. requested us to examine the one before us, which appeared to us to be beautifully executed. It exhibited the entire course of the ship from the Cape to the Arctic Sea, and her return to the spot where her gallant commander was murdered.

The islands discovered by Kerguelen seem to have been his first object, and afterwards New Holland and the Society Isles, and the archipelago to which his own name has been given. Continuing the course towards the north, he then touched the coast of America. This was in 1777. Then, passing through Behring's Straits, he thought he had attained his end, when he suddenly found himself prevented by ice from making farther progress. The route then altered towards Asia, and coasted Siberia. Here again a disappointment occurred, and the course was retraced, and was carried on to the Sandwich Islands, and the navigators were well received at Owaihe, and supplied with all they required. They sailed thence for Kamschatka, but this project being defeated by the loss of the mainmast in a gale of wind, they were obliged to return to Owaihe. *This* time, however, everything seemed changed! The natives now showed themselves in the character of traitors and robbers, and seized one of the boats. Captain Cook went to the chief to reclaim it, but on the road, being assaulted by one of the natives, he ordered him to be fired upon, and the man was killed. Having had occasion for fuel, Captain Cook's people had pulled down an old hut, as they thought it, but it unfortunately contained a fetish. The "sacrilege," as it was considered by the natives, and the death of the man who had been shot, excited the wrath of the islanders, who fell upon the captain and his four men and massacred them on the spot. All this of course is well known, but it was very interesting to hear it read from this journal with the actual map before us. " I know not," said Captain R, " whether it was in derision, or as a trophy of triumph, that they sent one of Captain Cook's fingers to my father, who had remained on board, the body itself having been cut to pieces."

The chart on which we traced out the voyage, while our friend was reading the journal to us, which I should observe was illustrated sometimes by pen and ink drawings, was so beautifully executed that I could not help expressing my surprise to see remain in private hands a document which would be the pride of any royal museum.

" It was," replied Captain R, " by a singular chance that it came into my possession. When my father transmitted these documents to George III. with a detailed report of the expedition, the King expressed so much satisfaction, that not content with making him a handsome present, he recompensed him further by promotion. My father crossed the royal threshold a simple mate, but he re-crossed it a first lieutenant. His career, which now looked so promising, was too soon at an end. At the age of thirty-six he was cut off by a fever while on a voyage on the western coast of Africa. The pensions bestowed on his widow and children evinced the estimation in which he was held. As to this chart, it had been so ill-used and torn that it was considered useless, and thrown aside accordingly. Happily I succeeded in obtaining it, and having always been a diligent student of geography, and possessing some talent for drawing, I took great pains to restore it to its original beauty and perfection. I afterwards made an exact copy of it, which I offered to the King, and for which he gave me £250, and authorised me to retain the original as a relic of my father."

Such was the interesting recital of our friend, and I could perceive that all the talent of the father had descended to the son. Garibaldi afterwards confirmed this, by telling me that

Captain R had more than once made rapid sketches of sites and military positions, which had been of great value. His services in the British navy were very important, which is proved by his having been offered the command of the Sardinian fleet, but he preferred retaining his independence.

Our evening was thus spent in a most amusing and instructive manner; and in taking leave of our good host, I said to him, " Bad as I fear the dinner I can offer you will be, I hope you will accept it, when I tell you that the General will be one of my guests."

" I would come," said he, " with the greatest pleasure, but my illness forbids it; nevertheless, I will send a representative in the shape of several things which will avail you for your banquet, and some wine, in which I hope you will drink to your ' absent friends,' not forgetting old Captain R among them."

CHAPTER IV.

A CAPRICE BEFORE DEPARTING.

I Should have begun to think that the last spark of eccentricity had been extinguished in me had I been able to quit these islands without for a moment touching the soil of Sardinia; and therefore, to the utter astonishment of my companion, and in total disregard of the mighty cares which burthened his mind with regard to the coming dinner-party, and obstinately bent on following my own caprice, I profited, by the fineness of the morning of the day fixed for our feast and our departure, to drag the reluctant captain to the beach as soon as the first streaks of daylight appeared in the East.

While the sailors were getting a boat ready, I remarked near the landing-place a bomb, fixed on a marble pedestal. This projectile I was told was preserved as a souvenir of the young Napoleon, who in 1793 fired it upon the island, when the French endeavoured to get possession. The future Emperor was then but a lieutenant of artillery.

A distance of about three English miles separates La Maddalena from Parau, the nearest point of Sardinia where a landing can be effected. Our boat went slowly from the shore, and we were able to admire the little town in its best aspect. The houses, of one and two stories, painted rose-colour and yellow and green, were raised around the natural amphitheatre. The hills, at the height of about 1,000 feet, are crowned with the forts Balbiano, GuardiaVecchia, Andrea, and Camicia. The clumps of flowers and shrubs which embellished the houses of the principal inhabitants, the miniature marine which enlivened the port, added to the smooth and azure sea, formed so happy and perfect a combination, that it looked as if a tempest could never have disturbed its tranquillity. A little later, when the sun had raised itself by degrees behind the isle of San Stefano, and I saw the bright light shining on the most beautiful spots, I felt so intensely the influence of the sweet climate aud the charm of this soli tude of nature, that I was overwhelmed with the sad thought that in a few more hours the " Virgilio" was to restore me to a life of comparative monotony.

It was under this impression that I began to try my powers at persuading Captain D of the propriety of deferring our return to Italy. I proposed to him to go by land to Porto Torres, and thence to proceed by next week's steamer to Genoa. With a view to shaking his resolves, I depicted to him in glowing colours the pleasure we should have in running over the mountainous region and the verdant valleys of La Gallura. I told him we might make a pilgrimage to the sanctuary of Logu Santu, celebrated for its church of the thirteenth century, where were the relics of Saints Nicholas and Trano. That we should be able to visit Tempio and la Punta, in Bellestreri—the principal point of the granite chain of Monte Limbara, where we should encounter the shepherd population, the "Gallegos" of Sardinia; and then follow the route to Sessari, where we could stop to view the " Sepolturas de is Gigantes," and the " Nurhags," as the Sardinians call some curious monuments which they believe to be sepulchres.

My descriptions were wasted, my efforts vain. I had to work upon a grey-headed sailor, and not on an adventurous knight; on a father of a family with plenty to do, and not on an idle tourist. I was obliged to console myself with a rapid glance at that little point of Sardinia where the keel of our boat grounded. Before us was the post station, Parau, where the horses of the last stage were allowed a short rest before returning: some of them were standing there now. Though of a good breed, they had a pitiful aspect. No care is taken of them. They held their heads low, and were left in the sun to dry the perspiration their journey had produced, while their tails were actively but ineffectually employed in whisking the flies which tormented them.

The transport of letters and passengers is so primitive and so wretchedly managed, that when the courier arrives at Parau, he seldom finds any means at hand of getting over to La Maddalena, and has to light a large fire as a signal for a boat to come over.

This northern corner of Sardinia offers nothing of any interest to a visitor. A solitary, wild and desolate plain stretches behind Parau. It is covered with bushes of broom and arbutus. Now and then you see a group of goats, whose wild looks plainly show that the approach of a stranger surprises and troubles them. A small party of horsemen, in picturesque costume, and armed to the teeth, brought to my mind similar rencontres in Sicily, in Greece, and in Barbary. I saw that La Gallura deserved its renown for smuggling and marauding, but I would willingly have braved such perils, could I have penetrated farther into the country.

After a brisk walk of three-quarters of an hour across these masses of bushes, bathed in the rays of the early morn, we arrived at the first hut of the peasants, perhaps I should say the *boors,* who are the sole inhabitants of this district. It was formed of some lumps of stone loosely piled. Flocks of sheep and goats, the former at liberty, the latter in pens round the house, formed the riches of the owner. Halfa-dozen dogs announced our arrival to the padrone, who came forth with his wife and children, and the herdsman. He saluted us with a dignified simplicity, and invited us to enter; and I thought to myself " one must go, nowadays, to the confines of the desert, to meet with that patriarchal hospitality, which it does one so much good to receive, showing us that the cordial manners of what we call the good old times still exist in some remote parts.

I was not a little surprised at the order and propriety of the interior of this poor dwelling. A large family-bed occupied one end of the room, and the rest was arranged as a kitchen with its various utensils around it. A few benches served for seats; a piece of mutton was boiling over a circle of heated stones in the middle of the room; and as there was no vent for the smoke but through the doorway, it was easy to imagine the case of these people when the weather obliged them to close the door: darkness and blindness, or cold and rain, must be their alternatives.

Having heard so much of the national costume of Sardinia, which is said to be that of the Phoenicians of old, I was very desirous of examining it. It may be more to be admired in the towns and villages, but all that I saw was miserable enough! The padrone and the herdsman wore the true dress of the country, as they told me. Their caps, their long vests, bound around with a girdle; their ample cloaks and their gaiters, all except their full linen trousers, were made of a coarse serge, called " furresi." Each family weaves this stuff for themselves out of the dark wool of their flocks. A vast quantity is thus produced in Gallura, but it is not exported.

The dress of a Sardinian is entirely wanting in the grace of form and the vivid colours which distinguish that of the Italians, whose costumes entirely harmonise with their gay and careless character.

The little time we had to spare wore rapidly away. A look from my companion, after inspecting his watch, recalled to my mind our approaching departure, and having distributed a few " muta " among the children, we retraced our steps to Parau.

For this time, dear reader, I will put your patience to no longer trial. I will not weary you with further descriptions of beauties, which raised in me such, overflowing admiration that I could not help expatiating upon them.

On our return to La Maddalena the sea was so smooth that we had to trust entirely to our oars, and to incite our rowers to every exertion to diminish the distance between us and the land as quickly as possible.

" You are just in time," cried Susini from the shore. " Your guests are all here; the

N ' dinner is ready; and as this fine weather will bring the Virgilio' here before her time, we have not a moment to lose."

We gave our friends a hurried reception, and begged them to enter our modest abode, and place themselves at once around the table of the Fazios, which doubtless had not been honoured with such an assembly since it commenced its career as a table.

If the banquet which f set before them was not all that an epicure could wish, at least it was done justice to by my friendly visitors; and the delightful conversation of the General, the broad humour of the Captain, and the good manners of my other friends, repaid my cares as amply as I could desire.

Towards the close of the repast Captain R came in, and no doubt many a tale and many a toast would have further prolonged our sitting, had not a messenger appeared to spoil our pleasure, by the announcement that the " Virgilio" was ready to start.

Her steam was up. The same boat which had brought us ashore a few days ago took us again on board, again impelled by the strong arm of the young Menotti.

With silent emotion the General pressed my hand, and before I was aware, he was gone.

This momentary streak of light in my existence had passed away, and the dimness of every-day life was to surround me once more.

THE END.

London: Printed by W. Clowes and Soks, 14, Charing Cfoss,

So, Conduit Street, Hanover Square.

Messrs. SAUNDERS, OTLEY, & Co.'s LITERARY ANNOUNCEMENTS.
THE VOYAGE of the NO VARA;
The Austrian Expedition Round the World." With upwards of 400 wood engravings. 3 vols., 8vo.
THE HISTORY OF THE CHURCH OF ENGLAND, from the Death of Elizabeth to the Present Time. By the Rev. Geo. G. Perry, M.A., Rector of Waddington, late Fellow of Lincoln College, Oxford. 3 vols., 8vo. THE LIFE AND WRITINGS of the RIGHT HON. BENJAMIN DISRAELI, M. P. THE LIFE OF GEORGE FOX,
The Founder of the Quakers. From numerous MSS., and other original sources. 10s. 6d.
THE TRAVELS AND ADVENTURES OF DR. WOLFF, the Bokhara Missionary. Dedicated to the Right Hon.
W. E. Gladstone, M.P. 1st. vol., 2d. edition, 18s. Second vol. 18s.

THE PRIVATE JOURNAL OF THE MARQUESS OF HASTINGS, Governor-General and
Commander-in-Chief in India.
Edited by his Daughter, Sophia, the Marchioness of Bute. Second
Edition, 2 vols, post 8vo, with Map and Index. 21s.
NAPOLEON THE THIRD ON ENGLAND.
Selections from his own writings. Translated by J. H. Simpson. 5s. RECOLLECTIONS OF GENERAL GARI BALDI; or, TRAVELS FROM ROME TO LUCERNE, comprising a Visit to the Mediterranean Islands of La Maddalena and Caprera. 10s. 6d.
THE HUNTING GROUNDS of the OLD WORLD. By H. A. L. (the Old Shekarry). Second Edition. 21s. HIGHLANDS AND HIGHLANDERS;
As they were and as they are. By William Grant Stewart. First and Second series, price 5s. each; extra bound, 6s. 6d.
THE ENGLISHMAN IN CHINA.
With numerous Woodcuts. 10s. 6d.
AN AUTUMN TOUR IN SPAIN.
By the Rev. R. Roeerts, Vicar of Melton Abbas, and of Trinity College,
Cambridge. With numerous Engravings. 21s.
LECTURES ON THE EPISTLE TO THE EPHESIANS. By the Rev. R. J.m'ghee. Second Edition. 2 vols,
Reduced price, 15s.
PRE-ADAMITE MAN; or, THE STORY OF OUR OLD PLANET AND ITS INHABITANTS, TOLD BY SCRIPTURE AND SCIENCE. Beautifully Illustrated by Hervieu, Dalziel Brothers, &c. 1 vol, post 8vo, 10s. 6d.
LOUIS CHARLES DE BOURBON; THE " PRISONER OF THE TEMPLE." 3.
A HANDY-BOOK for RIFLE VOLUNTEERS.
With 14 Coloured Plates and Diagrams. By Captain W. G. Hartley, author of " A New System of Drill." 7s. Cd.
RECOLLECTIONS of a WINTER CAMPAIGN IN INDIA, in 1857—58. By Captain Oliver J. Jones, R.N. With numerous illustrations drawn on'stone by Day, from the Author's Sketches. In 1 vol. royal 8vo, 16s. TWO YEARS IN SYRIA.
Ry T. Lewis Farley, Esq., Late Chief Accountant of the Ottoman
Bank, Beyrout. 12s. Second Edition.
DIARY of TRAVELS in THREE QUARTERS OF THE GLOBE. By an Australian Settler. 2 vols, post8vo,21s. MOUNT LEBANON and its INHABITANTS:
A Ten Years' Residence from 1842 to 1852. By Colonel Churchill, Staff Officer in the British Expedition to Syria. Second Edition 3 vols, 8vo, £1 5s. ' *Messrs. Saunders, Otley, & Co.'s Literary Announcements.* FROM SOUTHAMPTON TO CALCUTTA.
Sketches of Anglo-Indian Life. 10s. 6d.
TRAVEL and RECOLLECTIONS of TRAVEL.
By Dr. John Shaw. 1 vol, post 8vo, 7s. 6d.
LETTERS ON INDIA.
By Edward Sullivan, Esq., Author of ' Rambles in North and South
America;' ' The Bungalow and the Tent;' ' From Boulogne to Babel-Mandeb;' ' A Trip to the Trenches 5' &c. 1 vol. 7s.
CAMPAIGNING IN KAFFIRLAND; or, SCENES AND ADVENTURES IN THE KAFFIR WAR OF 1851—52. By Captain W. R. King. Second Edition. 1 vol. 8vo, 14s.
THE RELIGIOUS TENDENCIES OF THE AGE. 6s. 6d.
Mrs. JAMESON'S LIVES OF FEMALE SOVEREIGNS. Third Edition. 21s.
Mrs. JAMESON'S CHARACTERISTICS OF WOMEN. New Library Edition. On Fine Tinted Paper, with illustrations from the Author's Designs. 2 vols, post 8vo, 21s.
ADVENTURES OF A GENTLEMAN IN SEARCH OF A HORSE. By Sir George Stephen. With illustrations by Cruikshank. Sixth Edition, 7s. 6d. THE LANGUAGE OF FLOWERS,
Elegant Gift Book for the Season. Beautifully bound in green watered silk, with coloured plates. Containing the Art of Conveying Sentiments of Esteem and Affection.
" By all those token Bowers, which tell What words can never speak so well."—*Byron*. Eleventh edition, dedicated, by permission, to the Duchess of Kent. 10s. 6d.
THE MANAGEMENT OF BEES;
With a description of the " Ladies' Safety Hive." By Samdel BagSter, Jun. 1 vol., illustrated. 7s.
THE HANDBOOK OF TURNING,
With numerous plates. A complete and Practical Guide to the Beautiful Science of Turning in all its Branches. 1 vol. 7s. 6d.
TEXTS FOR TALKERS.
By Frank Fowler. 3s. fid.
The SUMMER TOUR of an INVALID. 5s. 6d. THE NEWSPAPER PRESS OF THE PRESENT DAY. Is. 6d.
ARMY MISRULE; BARRACK THOUGHTS.
By a Common Soldier. 3s. *JFittion.*
CRISPIN KEN.
By the Author of' Miriam May.' Dedicated, by special permission, to the Right Hon. Sir E. B. Lytton, Bart., M.P. 10s. 6d.
WHO SHALL BE DUCHESS? or, THE NEW LORD OF BURLEIGH. A Novel. 2 vols., 21s. THE LIGHTHOUSE. A Novel. 2 vols. , 21s. THE SKELETON IN THE CUPBOARD. By Lady Scott. 2 vols. 21s.
TOO LATE.
By Mrs. Dimsdale. Dedicated, by permission, to Right Hon. Sir E.
B. Lytton, Bart., M.P. 7s. 6d.
WHY PAUL FERROLL KILLED HIS WIFE.
By the Author of " Paul Ferroll." Third Edition. 10s. 6d.
The RECTOR'S DAUGHTERS, i vol., ios. 6d. HELEN. A Romance of Real Life. 7s. 6d. GERTRUDE MELTON; or, NATURE'S NOBLEMAN. A Tale. 7s. 6d.
MY WIFE'S PINMONEY.
By E. E. Nelson, a grand niece of the great Lord Nelson. 5s.
THE EMIGRANT'S DAUGHTER.
Dedicated, by permission, to the Empress of Russia. 5s.
Messrs. Saunders, Otley, & Co.'s Literary Announcements. MIRIAM MAY. th Edition, ios. 6d.
WHISPERING VOICES OF THE YULE.
Tales for Christmas. 5s.
THE SENIOR FELLOW.
A Tale of Clerical Life. 10s. 6d.
ALMACK'S.
A Novel. Dedicated to the Ladies Patronesses of the Balls at Aimack's. New Edition, 1 vol, crown 8vo, 10s. 6d.

NELLY CAREW.
By Miss Power. 2 vols, 21s.
MEMOIRS of a LADY IN WAITING.
By the Author of 'Adventures of Mrs. Colonel Somerset in Caffraria.' 2 vols, 18s.
HULSE HOUSE.
A Novel. By the Author of ' Anne Gray. ' 2 vols, post 8vo, 21s.
THE NEVILLES OF GARRETSTOWN.
A Historical Tale. Edited, and with a Preface by the Author of
'Emilia Wyndham.' 3 vols, post 8vo, 31s. 6d.
CORVODA ABBEY.
A Tale. 1 vol, post 8vo, 10s. 6d.
THE VICAR OF LYSSEL.
The Diary of a Clergyman in the 18th century. 4s. 6(1.
GOETHE IN STRASBOURG.
A Dramatic Nouvelette. By H. Noel Humphreys. 7s. 6d.
ROTTEN ROW. A Novel, *i* vols., 21s.
SQUIRES AND PARSONS.
A Church Novel. 1 vol. 10s. 6d.
THE DEAN; or, the POPULAR PREACHER.
By Berkeley Aikin, Author of ' Anne Sherwood.' 3 vols, post 8vo, 31s. 6d.
CHARLEY NUGENT; or, PASSAGES IN THE LIFE OF A SUB. A Novel, 3 vols, post 8vo, 31s. 6d. PAUL FERROLL.
By the Author of ' IX Poems by V.' Fourth Edition. Post 8vo, lOs. 6d.
SWEETHEARTS AND WIVES.
By Marooerite A. Power. A Novel. 3 vols., 31s. 6d.
The LOOSE SCREW. A Novel. 3 vols. , 31s. 6d. LADY AUBREY; or, WHAT SHALL I DO? By the Author of ' Every Day.' A. Novel. 2vols,2Js.
THE IRONSIDES.
A Tale of the English Commonwealth. 3 vols., 31s. 6d.
AGNES HOME. A Novel, ios. 6d.
LA CAVA; or,
RECOLLECTIONS OF THE NEAPOLITANS 10s. 6d. ANSELMO.
A Tale of Modern Italy. 2 vols., 21s.
THE DALRYMPLES; or, LONG CREDIT AND LONG CLOTH. 0s. 6d. INSTINCT AND REASON.
By Lady Julia Lockwood. 5s.
The HISTORY of ELMIRE DE ST. CLAIRE, during the period of her Residence in the Country with a Clergyman's Family. A Tale of Real Life.
AN M.P. IN SEACH OF A CREED.
A Novel. 10s. 6d.
CARELADEN HOUSE. A Novel, ios. 6d.
Sir E. L. Bulwer's Eva, AND OTHER POEMS.
Earl Godwin's Feast, AND OTHER POEMS. By Stewart Lockyer.
Messrs. Saunders, Otley, & Co.'s Literary Announcements.
Saint Bartholomew's Day, AND OTHER. POEMS. By Stewart Lockyer.
Sacred Poems.
By the late Bright Hon. Sir Robert Grant, with a Notice by Lord Glenelg.
Eustace;
An Elegy. By the Right Hon. Charles Tennyson D'Eyncourt.
The Pleasures of Home.
By the Rev. J. T. Campbell.
Friendship; AND OTHER POEMS. By Hierrnicos. 5s.
Judith; AND OTHER POEMS. By Francis Mills, M.R.C.S.L. 5s.
The Convert, AND OTHER POEMS. 5s.
Oberon's Empire.
A Mask.
The Spirit of Home.
By Sylvan.
The Moslem and the Hindoo.
A Poem on the Sepoy Revolt. By a Graduate of Oxford.
Palmam, qui Meruit, Ferat.
By Norman B. Yonge.
Miscellaneous Poems.
By an Indian Officer.
The Shadow of the Yew, AND OTHER POEMS. By Norman B. Yonge.
Carmagnola.
An Italian Tale of the Fifteenth Century.
Hanno.
A Tragedy. The Second Edition.
EAST INDIA ARMY, COLONIAL AND GENERAL AGENCY. 50, Conduit Street, Hanover Square, Londjon.
(Close to the " Oriental Club.")
Messrs. Saunders, Otley, and Co. beg to announce that in consequence of their daily increasing relations with India, Australia, and the Colonies, they have opened an East India Army, Colonial, and General Agency, in connection with their long-established Publishing House, and they take this opportunity to invite the attention of Regimental Messes, Officers, Members of the Civil Service, and other Residents in India, Australia, and the Colonies thereto, and to the advantages it offers.
BANKING DEPARTMENT.
Pat, Pensions, Fond Allowances, Dividends, &c, drawn and remitted with regularity. Sales of, and Investments in, Govern ment Stock, Foreign Securities, &c, effected. Every other description of Financial Business transacted.
SUPPLY DEPARTMENT.
Miscellaneous Supplies Of Every Description, including Provisions, Wines, Plate, Jewellery, Books, Guns, Band Instruments, Clothing, &c, carefully selected and despatched by Overland Route, or Sailing Ship, to Regiments and Messes in India, Australia, and the Colonies.
Private Orders from Officers, Members of the Civil Service, and Residents in India, Australia, and the Colonies generally, are executed with care, economy, efficiency, and promptitude.
All orders should be accompanied by full and detailed directions.
PERSONAL AGENCY DEPARTMENT.
The Constituents of Messrs. Saunders, Otley, and Co. may depend upon receiving every attention to their requirements and instructions. Every assistance will be afforded to their Constituents and their Families on their arrival in England, with the view to relieve them from every possible inconvenience.
Charge, when required, will be taken of children coming from India and the Colonies, and arrangements will be made for their education in England.
To those going out to In jia, Australia, and the Colonies, Messrs. Saunders, Otley, and Co. r/fer their services to secure passages Overland, or by Ship, and to afford them all necessary information connected therewith.
All Letters, Parcel, &c, will be received by Messrs. Saunders, Otley, and Co., for t'jeir Constituents (whether in England, India, or the Colonies), to ',/ iom they will be forwarded regularly.
TERMS.

No Commission Charged on the execution of Orders, whether from Regimental Messes or Private Individuals, When Accompanied By A Remittance, and a small Discount at all times allowed.